100 Prayers for Daily Living in Modern Culture

U Got 2 Pray

Fr. Stan Fortuna, C.F.R.

Our Sunday Visitor Publishing Division
Our Sunday Visitor, Inc.
Huntington, Indiana 46750

W9-AVL-609

Nihil Obstat: Rev. Michael Heintz
Censor Librorum

Imprimatur: ✠ John M. D'Arcy
Bishop of Fort Wayne-South Bend
December 22, 2003

Unless otherwise noted, the Scripture citations contained herein are from the *Holy Bible, New International Version* (NIV), copyright © 1973, 1978, 1984 by the International Bible Society. Used by permission. All rights reserved.

Scripture citations noted as RSV are taken from the *Catholic Edition of the Revised Standard Version of the Bible* (RSV), copyright © 1965 and 1966 by the Division of Christian Education of the National Council of the Churches of Christ in the United States of America. Used by permission. All rights reserved.

Every reasonable effort has been made to determine copyright holders of excerpted materials and to secure permissions as needed. If any copyrighted materials have been inadvertently used in this work without proper credit being given in one form or another, please notify Our Sunday Visitor in writing so that future printings of this work may be corrected accordingly.

Our Sunday Visitor Publishing Division
Our Sunday Visitor, Inc.
200 Noll Plaza
Huntington, IN 46750

ISBN: 1-931709-96-3 (Inventory No. T53)
LCCN: 2003113175

Cover design by Tyler Ottinger
Interior design by Sherri L. Hoffman
Interior art by Andy Kurzen

PRINTED IN THE UNITED STATES OF AMERICA

This book is dedicated to:
Pope John Paul II
– my hero –
a prayin man 4 real.

Table of Contents

Foreword

Praying with a group of friends a little over a year ago on New Year's Eve, I felt that God spoke to me. It was a strange word — different from things I had heard from Him before. I heard Him say, "Get out of the shadows." I spent the next several weeks trying to figure out what "shadow" I was in. My first interpretation was that I was in some kind of personal sin, or maybe under the influence of something evil. It made sense to me that a shadow was dark, so it must be something evil. Right?

After several weeks of praying and questioning, one day I finally made a breakthrough. For some reason I started remembering all the powerful things that I had experienced in my life, even recently. If I was in an evil shadow, then it wasn't separating me completely from God's power. So what was this shadow? I started looking for the word "shadow" in the Scriptures, and I was surprised with what I found.

Most of the references to a shadow were not about evil, but about protection — "In the shadow of your wings," "In the shadow of the Almighty," etc. There was even a reference in the New Testament where people tried to get into Peter's shadow in order to be healed. I started looking at this word in a whole new way. What if the shadow was God's shadow? What if the shadow was a good thing, but

God was just calling me out from it for something better?

It took me several months to finally understand where God was taking me. I remember praying one day and finally understanding the rest of this new direction God was revealing to me. I felt He was saying to me, "You've been in my shadow your whole life. And that's not a bad place to be. You have experienced many miracles, you have seen great power, you have tasted true joy. But now I want you to come out of my shadow, and into my radiance. I want you to come before my face, where I can look on you, and you can see my glory."

Wow! What a concept! To think that I had all these experiences in my relationship with Christ and in prayer, and now there was still so much more! It gave me a new hunger for prayer, just to spend time in Jesus' presence.

And that's not really my style. My tendency is to always "do" something before I spend time in prayer. There are always so many things that need to be done. And I can be pretty convincing to myself about how those things are sometimes more important than even prayer. But a lesson that I have learned the hard way is that without prayer, I can't "DO" anything. Prayer is the fuel. It's the energy source, the sustaining force. "I am the vine; YOU are the branches . . . apart from me, you can do NOthing" (John 15:5, emphasis added).

Do you want to make an impact with your life? Pray! Want to make a difference in this world? Pray! Want to be a big player for God — someone He comes to when there is a need? Pray! Want to be a part of a revolution springing forth from today's generation of teens and young adults? Pray!

It's like St. Paul says, "Rejoice in your hope, be patient in tribulation, be constant in prayer" (Romans 12:12, RSV). Constant! That's a huge challenge. Most of us struggle with praying for a few minutes every day, let alone constantly! So how do we do it? How do we respond to this?

The New Testament is filled with references about prayer. We see everything from how Jesus prayed to Him, teaching us to pray with the Our Father. Prayer is obviously one of the foundation stones of the believer's new life.

This book that Fr. Stan has written offers an incredible resource to teens and young adults to help them bring this challenge to life. The book has covered every topic imaginable. Need a prayer for some situation in your life, but just can't find the right words? *U Got 2 Pray* has the words for you, and a hinge to a Scripture passage to go with it! For almost any circumstance you could encounter, there is a prayer here for you.

This isn't one of those books you read straight through like a novel. I picture this being one of the books I carry around with me all the time, jumping through it from topic to topic as the need arises, leading me to prayer in the moments I need to be there the most. You may want to get another copy now, because you will probably wear this one out!

I pray that every person that uses this book will come to a deeper experience of prayer. And I pray that you will come out of the shadows yourself, and more into the radiance of God's presence, where He can look on you and you can experience His glory.

JIM BECKMAN
Director of Catechesis
International LIFE TEEN Program

"Do not be anxious about anything, but in everything, by prayer and petition, with thanksgiving, present your requests to God" (Philippians 4:6).

જ

Introduction

I originally intended this introduction to be really long, almost a second book "on prayer," a collection of thoughts and teachings "about prayer" from many saints, masters, and experts on the subject. After prayin about that and thinkin about that, along with a little help from my editor, I plainly and simply want this introduction to be like this book – not about prayer, but 110% plus about prayin – U got 2 pray!

This book is not a manual to read about prayer, it is a manual of prayers to be prayed. There's a difference, and I pray you get it. I'm sure I could have come up with some awesome stuff "about prayer." I've got tons of material, and there's plenty of really important, good, and even great books out there about prayer. I was even gonna include a "readin list" of some of these books about prayer that are out there in the appendix. Instead, we're includin an appendix of more prayers – wonderful traditional prayers to be prayed. U got 2 pray!

This book of "composed" prayers with accompanying Scriptures flowed from my heart while I was prayin. The point of puttin together a book of prayers is to hopefully provide the reader with an inspiring opportunity to make the transition from readin to prayin in a regular and effective way. It is my intention to make this book of prayers a culturally relevant collection that can be intelligible to the human person – young and old – livin in a cultural climate that is hostile to spiritual values and unresponsive to the critical and urgent need for us to pray. Thus, *U Got 2 Pray.*

As in my previous book, *U Got 2 Believe!*, the linguistic style of this book includes contemporary phrases of urban slang in both content and "spellin." Please know that this is intentional and not the result of poor copy editing! In his message for World Mission Sunday, the Holy Father Pope John Paul II said, "A new apostolic outreach is needed . . . taking into account each person's needs in regard to their sensitivity and language." I'm hopin the language and style of this book will reach out to the hearts and sensitivities of you, its readers, to help you feel and make a generous response and commitment to the critical and urgent need for us to pray in the first place, and hopefully to do so with greater regularity and intensity.

If this book doesn't get you prayin, it has failed, so let's get right to it.

Let us pray:

O God, I pray to You as I write this introduction; I pray for and I pray with whoever is readin it with me as I write it right now – Lord, teach us to pray and take us deeper into Your mystery. Help us to be less concerned and worried about prayer and more and more focused on and committed to simply prayin; give us Your gift of peace, the peace that every person desperately needs and yearns for, the peace that is beyond all understandin, the peace necessary to live in modern culture which confronts us with ever new and more difficult challenges every day. Let this peace fill our hearts and overflow to the hearts of all peoples in every culture, everywhere, right now. Teach us to pray always, in different ways, at all times, for different reasons, and even for no reason other than just to be with You, to have peace and to live with and to love one another. Thank You, Lord . . . Amen.

See what I'm sayin?

One Way to Pray This Book

So, how do you use this book? Pray. How do you pray?

#1. Open your heart and say, "Holy Spirit, come into my heart and lead me to the prayer You want me to pray right now."

#2. Open the book and pray the first prayer you lay your eyes on, or let prayer flow from the Scripture you read. Maybe you're flippin through this book somewhere wonderin if you should buy it, or maybe you already bought it, or maybe someone gave you the book and said, "You got to check this book out." It doesn't matter. All that matters is that you pray. U got 2 pray!

If you did what I just said, prayed to the Holy Spirit and opened the book and felt the prayer or Scripture or whatever wasn't speakin to you, remember you're suposta be prayin — givin, not gettin. Maybe, at this time, you won't be prayin the prayer for yourself, maybe you're meant to be prayin for someone else. That doesn't matter either, just pray. Sometimes we got to move beyond what we feel, and prayer is the key to get that motion goin, and prayer will keep it goin. The only thing that matters with this book is that it gets you prayin. If there's anything we need in our modern culture right now, and if there's anything the people livin in the midst of this modern culture need right now, it's prayer. We need a prayin people. That means we need people who pray, people who learn how to pray from prayin — U got 2 pray!

The Scriptures and some other texts provided on every page that precede all the prayers in this book are tremendous sources to inspire you, challenge you, and lead you to prayer. As a matter of fact, all the prayers in this book were born from and flow from the provided Scriptures. The Bible, the revealed word of God, inspired by the Holy Spirit, is the undisputed, everlastin wellspring, flowin unceasingly with inspiration, motivation, and power for prayer.

The Holy Spirit Himself is the master of prayer, and it is He who ultimately teaches, inspires, and sustains prayer in the heart and life of the one who prays. Hopefully that's you and me. Don't worry about how prayer is gonna happen; don't even worry about your weakness no matter what it is (or what they are!); in fact don't worry at all — just trust. Trust in the Holy Spirit that prayer will happen, and give Him permission to let it happen, and then "hold on" for the ride, or more accurately, "let go" and enjoy the true freedom that comes when we trust in and surrender to the Holy Spirit: "The Spirit helps us in our weakness. We do not know what we ought to pray for, but the Spirit himself intercedes for us with groans that words cannot express. And he who searches our hearts knows the mind of the Spirit, because the Spirit intercedes for the saints in accordance with God's will" (Romans 8:26–27). Alleluia . . . see what I'm sayin? So let's trust in the Holy Spirit; we can't go wrong, there's no excuse — U got 2 pray!

Another Way to Pray This Book

Another way to use this book is to browse through the table of contents and see if any of the chapter or prayer titles move your heart. Havin the heart moved, sensin some kinda inspiration, is very much a part of the beginning of prayer. It can happen with this book, and it can happen anywhere, any time, any place, and with any and every event no matter how good or bad, no matter how ugly or beautiful. Maybe as your eyes pass over the words of the chapter titles – day, night, relationships, work, struggle, victory, mystery, faith, hope, love – somethin might touch your heart. Follow up on that inspiration. It will get you prayin. It might be some of the titles of the prayers themselves that move you or challenge you to pray, like: #10 Driving & Public Transportation, #19 Prayer 4 the World, #27 Myself; or maybe #40 Serious Life Project, #47 Lies and the Truth, #51 Willingness 2 Suffer; or maybe #67 The

Street, #79 The Dark Night of Faith, or #88 New Creation – New Culture. When you check out the table
of contents there are 100 prayers aimed at helpin
you to pray and live in modern culture in a way that
will make a positive difference. U got 2 pray!

A Prayin People

My hero, Pope John Paul II, said somethin really
awesome about what's needed today in the heart of
the Church and the heart of the world – the heart
of modern culture. He said, "What is needed is a
Christian life distinguished above all in the art of
prayer. In as much as contemporary culture, even
amid so many indications to the contrary, has wit-
nessed the flowering of a new call for spirituality,
due also to the influence of other religions, it is
more urgent than ever that our Christian communities should become 'genuine schools of prayer.'"

The art of prayer, that's the key. That is, prayers
prayed in the lives of a prayerful and devoted prayin
people; individuals, communities, families, parishes,
and neighborhoods becomin "genuine schools of
prayer" – places where there are prayin people.
That's what this book is about, to get people prayin,
makin progress and becomin familiar with and in
love with the art of prayer and even more so in love
with the One to whom we pray; makin the "genuine
school of prayer" thing somethin 4 real. More
prayer . . . more love, more love . . . more peace – U
got 2 pray!

This book is intended to be a small help towards that end; that is, makin the art of prayer accessible to people of all cultures and ages by helpin them to pray more deeply and more frequently, more faithfully and fruitfully, becomin vibrant contributors wherever they live to makin their communities, families, parishes – whatever and wherever – genuine schools of prayer; to help us become and stay a prayin people 4 real. This book is dedicated to Pope John Paul II – my hero – a prayin man 4 real.

Believin and prayin are kinda like "two peas in a pod," but if the believin and prayin don't lead to love – if we don't become people filled with and livin with more love – then "we ain't nothin" (check out 1 Corinthians 13). So as a result, please keep your eye out for, and pray for me as I begin to work on, my next book, *U Got 2 Love*.

Please pray for me, be sure of my prayer for you and know that "I kneel before the Father, from whom his whole family in heaven and on earth derives its name. I pray that out of his glorious riches he may strengthen you with power through his Spirit in your inner being, so that Christ may dwell in your hearts through faith. And I pray that you, being rooted and established in love, may have power, together with all the saints, to grasp how wide and long and high and deep is the love of Christ, and to know this love that surpasses knowledge – that you may be filled to the measure of all the fullness of God. Now to him who is able to do immeasurably more than all we ask or imagine, according to his power at work within us, to him be glory in the church and in Christ Jesus throughout all generations, for ever and ever! Amen" (Ephesians 3:14–21).

Peace and blessings to you and your family and friends, now and 4 ever, in Jesus and Mary.

FATHER STAN FORTUNA, C.F.R.

CHAPTER 1

Day

Upon Waking A.M. Offering

"Guide me in your truth and teach me, for you are God my Savior, and my hope is in you all day long" (Psalm 25:5).

Heavenly Father, thank You for this new day. As I rise and enter this new day, before I fully wake up, I offer it all to You. As You brought me safely through the night, be with me and bring me safely through all that awaits me in this day. May my safe passage through the night give me confidence to trust that You will provide me with all I need and will direct the course of this day. May no person or thing, nor yesterday or tomorrow, distract me from You being with me today — right now in my first waking moments. Receive my heart, my mind, my body and my soul, so I can be overjoyed knowing by experience that You are in control. Find me ready to receive what You give me, as You give it to me and when You give it to me. Be my strength just for today, so I can stand fast to endure joyfully whatever may come. May Your goodness to me this day overflow and be a source of blessing for others and for all. Thank You . . .

Morning Offering ii

"By day the LORD directs his love, at night his song is with me – a prayer to the God of my life" (Psalm 42:8).

Lord Jesus, help me to do what I got to do today. Give me a sense of what the Father's will is, so that I may be strengthened and energized as if the Father's will was my food as it was for You: "'My food,' said Jesus, 'is to do the will of him who sent me and to finish his work'" (John 4:34). Jesus, I offer to You the entire day, especially all the details of my duties and responsibilities, along with all the frustrations and struggles. By Your grace may I finish His work just for today and bear abundant fruit for the glory of the Father and the good of Your Church. May this food not only be my strength but my greatest pleasure and delight. May the Father bring to completion the good work He has given me to do this day. I love You, Jesus . . .

Morning Offering iii

"Then will I ever sing praise to your name and fulfill my vows day after day" (Psalm 61:8).

Holy Spirit, may the blessing of this fresh new morning light shining forth from this new day cause me to be open to the power of Your divine light. May Your divine light mark out the path I must follow this day, strengthening me for sacrifice — for the sacrifice of divine love lived out in all the details and events that await me this day. Holy Spirit, fill me with the fire of Your love. Be my divine protection, my unfailing source of wisdom and strength to face Satan and all his evil and deceiving spirits throughout this day. May all my weaknesses be a cause for rejoicing because Your power is made perfect in weakness. Come Holy Spirit, Lord and Giver of Life, and make me shine, make me holy this day. Come Holy Spirit...

4

Daily Scripture & Eucharist

"Every word of God is flawless; he is a shield to those who take refuge in him" (Proverbs 30:5).

Lord Jesus help me to create a space sometime today, to somehow make some time so I can hear a word from You — from Your holy Gospel. Your Church provides me with a taste every day. Help me to take advantage of these daily readings from the word of God. If that don't work, help me to pray to the Holy Spirit to strengthen my willingness to hear You speaking to me today by opening up the Bible. Better still, along with this, arouse a hunger in me to go to Mass during the week at least one day so that the powerful two-punch combo of Your word and Your Body, Blood, Soul and Divinity can captivate me and transform me. Be my shield as I take refuge in You. Thank You, Jesus . . .

Life @ Home

"Even the sparrow has found a home, and the swallow a nest for her self, where she may have her young – a place near your altar, O LORD Almighty, my King and my God" (Psalm 84:3).

Lord Jesus, You were homeless when You were born in a manger in a stranger's barn. Later on, You had an awesome home life in Nazareth with Your mother, Mary, and Your foster father, Joseph. During Your public ministry, You told us that You did not have a place to lay Your head: "Foxes have holes and birds of the air have nests, but the Son of Man has no place to lay his head" (Matthew 8:20). So, in spite of all the conditions of my home life, even if I feel I don't have one, or if in reality I don't have one, I know that You can make me have one. So many people who live in houses have no home. Please bless them and all lonely hearts. Somehow make me feel at home in this life and fill me with Your love so I can help others feel the same way. Help me to belong. I know You can make improvements where no improvements are possible, because with You I believe all things are possible. Strengthen my faith. Do with me what You will. Be the difference in my life and make me make a difference in my home life. Jesus, You are with me always, and for this I thank You . . .

Life @ School

"The Counselor, the Holy Spirit, whom the Father will send in my name, will teach you all things and will remind you of everything I have said to you" (John 14:26).

Holy Spirit, Jesus promised that You would remind me of all the things He said and did. I trust in Your divine help. These lessons are the real lessons that give meaning to life. Instruct me in this school of life so that I will be found more readily available to learn, receiving the knowledge and wisdom that comes from Your inspiration. May the hard work, hours, and years of my formal education be opportunities for wisdom. Help me to be grateful for the commitment of my teachers and for the privilege to be in school. Bless all the many people who do not have the opportunity for formal education. Bless them with the wisdom and peace that comes from You. Bless all the members of my family, my neighborhood and my village, all my friends, all nations and cultures with the wisdom that makes us live in solidarity. Increase in me reverence and respect for all who have somethin to teach me. Make me a good student, a good listener and learner. Enlighten my mind to be critical of all the culture has to offer and empower my heart to be compassionate. Strengthen me not to complain when confronted with difficult lessons that might compromise truth. Conquer my pride and reveal to me that every person and event I encounter every day has somethin to teach me. Thank You Holy Spirit . . .

Life @ Work

"All hard work brings a profit, but mere talk leads only to poverty" (Proverbs 14:23).

"One who is slack in his work is brother to one who destroys" (Proverbs 18:9).

Heavenly Father, may all the work I do begin with Your inspiration and continue with Your saving help. Whatever I am called to do today, may I do it generously. Energize me to overcome all temptations to laziness and half-heartedness. Strengthen me to work hard. Help me to recognize the dignity of human work and to be mindful of the many people who have no work or who can't work. May the way I go about my work be pleasing to You; may I be pleasing to You. Help me to transform the workplace and whatever I do today with a greater knowledge and experience of being a co-worker with You. Increase my awareness of the dignity of both work and worker. Help me to sanctify the workplace wherever that may be today. May this solidarity be real and effective so that Your kingdom may be built up a little more each day starting with today. May our work always find its beginning in You and through You reach its completion. Thank You, Father . . .

Cleaning Up

"Nothing outside a man can make him 'unclean' by going into him. Rather, it is what comes out of a man that makes him 'unclean'" (Mark 7:15).

Lord Jesus, You said, "Blessed are the pure in heart" (Matthew 5:8). Help me this day to be aware of and responsive to all that needs to be cleaned up and put away. Expand my heart and purify my heart to see and do what needs to be done, wherever and whenever it needs to be done, piece-by-piece, event-by-event, person-by-person, day-by-day. Whether it be in my room, my studies, my prayer, my past, my family, my friends, the culture or, most especially, my heart . . . everything. Please help me to be aware of what needs to be done on the outside as well as on the inside. Help me to clean up the inside first, so the things on the outside will be able to take care of themselves with greater dependence on the gifts and fruits of the Holy Spirit. May the joy of finishing the many little tasks awaiting me this day prepare me and strengthen me for the bigger tasks. With You I can do all things. Help me to remain in You . . . Thank You, Jesus . . .

9

Language & Speech

"*To fear the* LORD *is to hate evil; I hate pride and arrogance, evil behavior and perverse speech*" (Proverbs 8:13).

Lord Jesus, You told us that "men will have to give an account on the day of judgment for every careless word they have spoken" (Matthew 12:36). Help me to use the gifts of language and speech in a way that is worthy of a child of God. Help me to communicate with the contemporary culture in a way that can be understood so that the message of the Gospel can penetrate and purify the culture. Take away all the fears that would make me be a coward rather than a courageous leader in the midst of my family and friends with regard to the way I speak and use language. Help me blaze a trail in the cultural verbal pollution that comes from so many different media and entertainment sources. Help me be careful and discerning with regard to the things I read and listen to, especially choices of music and movies, so I can be influenced by what is good and positive. Lord Jesus, purify my heart so that the words that flow out of my mouth may be purified. I remember what You said: "Out of the overflow of the heart the mouth speaks" (Matthew 12:34). Lord Jesus, purify my heart . . .

10

Driving & Public Transportation

"Even as he walks along the road, the fool lacks sense and shows everyone how stupid he is" (Ecclesiastes 10:3).

O God, as I go from place to place today I ask Your blessing of safety for all travelers by land, sea or air. Whether I drive myself or am driven by another, help us all to be careful, kind and courteous. If I take a subway, bus, or taxi, and for all people who travel by any other public means in every culture, please help us to be patient and work towards building a culture of solidarity. Please guide and direct our thoughts, words and actions, so that as we make our way to our short-term destinations, the long-term destination of heaven will be kept in view. Regardless of my means of transportation today, help me to conduct myself in the way of wisdom, avoiding the easy path of the fool. Please help me learn the lessons You wish to teach me today. Thank You, Jesus . . . Amen . . .

CHAPTER II
Night

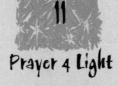

11

Prayer 4 Light

"Light is sweet, and it pleases the eyes to see the sun"
(Ecclesiastes 11:7).

Most high and glorious God, enlighten the darkness of my heart and the darkness of the culture. Put within me a correct faith, a certain hope and a perfect love that will shine in the darkness of this world and not be overcome by it. Give me a sense and a knowledge that will enable me to do Your holy will. Protect me from the way of the wicked, which is like deep darkness blinding them from what makes them stumble. Help me to live by truth, and come to me as the light of life. May Your word be the light on my path so that I may not stumble. Help me to be a child of the light, alert and self-controlled. Amen . . .

12

Entertainment

"Delight yourself in the LORD and he will give you the desires of your heart" (Psalm 37:4).

Lord, guide my choices of entertainment. Guide my choices in the midst of a multitude of options. There are so many different things to divert my mind and all my faculties from the stress, challenges and burdens of my responsibilities. May these diversions never take me away from You. Help me to choose good things to hold my attention — friends, music, movies, books, games, sports and whatever else can be used in a positive way for pleasure and relaxation. May my choices of entertainment renew my mind, body, soul, and spirit for a more faithful and fruitful life with You. Help me to delight in You and the good things that reflect Your Glory. Amen . . .

13
Before a Date

"Encourage the young men to be self-controlled. In everything set them an example by doing what is good" (Titus 2:6).

Come Holy Spirit deep into my heart, mind, and body; come deep into my bones, revealing the truth that it is for freedom that Jesus has set us free. As I prepare to go on this date, help both of us, and all who will be going out on dates tonight, not to be burdened by a yoke of slavery — slavery to the senses and a cultural standard that does not respect, accept, or promote purity and self-mastery. May the natural downward desires and energies of the sinful nature which leads to sexual impurity and immorality be influenced and elevated by Your supernatural power. Help us set high standards — show us how to live them. Holy Spirit, may Your power be perfected in all our weaknesses, and may Your presence in our bodies — Your temple — help us practice self control and strive for true and pure love with respect and dignity. Amen . . .

14

For the Lost & Lonely

"God sets forth the lonely in families, he leads forth the prisoners with singing; but the rebellious live in a sun scorched land" (Psalm 68:6).

Lord Jesus, the troubles of many hearts multiply each day. Turn to those and be gracious to those who are lost and feel lonely. Give them the grace to turn to You, because Your yoke is easy and Your burden light. Help them to know they are not alone, that You are with them always, even till the end of time. As they experience the pain and darkness of feeling lonely, help them to know they are not alone because of my prayer for them and my attitude and actions toward the lonely people I encounter along the way. Give us all a greater sense of communion and solidarity with You and with all peoples working to create a culture of solidarity.

15

For the Hopeless & Despairing

"From my youth I have been afflicted and close to death; I have suffered your terrors and am in despair" (Psalm 88:15).

Lord Jesus, there is no greater victory for the devil than to have someone hopeless and despairing, to have no sense of expectation and confidence. The ultimate victory of love You achieved for us is the key to defeating all hopelessness and despair, to give us confidence that we are not alone in spite of and along with all the many different things we feel. Increase within me a trust in You that will urge me to rely on You more and more day by day — to have a sense that with Your help I can fulfill the Father's will for me just for today. Keep me goin, Lord, and help me hold my head up just for today . . . Thank You, Jesus . . .

16

For the Homeless & Hungry

"Foxes have holes and birds of the air have nests, but
the Son of Man has no place to lay his head"
(Luke 9:58).

Lord Jesus, please forgive my lack of gratitude for the place I have to lay my head and the food I have to eat. Forgive me for all the times I complain about what I have and do not have, even if I'm really strugglin because I don't have what I want or what I think I need. Please help me to be more aware that You spent most of Your time out on the open road. Please help me to be aware of the many people who are so much worse off than I am. Most especially, instill within me an awareness of Your hidden presence in the homeless and the hungry. Give me the courage to show respect for them, acknowledging them as my brothers and sisters, as an expression of my love for You. Help me to be courageous and generous in assisting them in their need, because whatever I do or don't do for them I do or don't do for You. Lord Jesus, have mercy . . .

17

For Those Trapped in Sin

"I am the gate; whoever enters through me will be saved. He will come in and go out, and find pasture" (John 10:9).

Lord Jesus, sometimes it's so easy to be prevented from passing from one moment to the next, from one event to the next, from one day to the next in peace. This inner restriction is so difficult to break out of. Sin, with all its many different names and faces, has such a consistent capacity to trap us. To be delivered from this evil is the glory of Your coming in the flesh and of our being in relationship with You. Bless us with the peace of the "daily bread" that You taught us to pray for and the deliverance from evil and all sin. Help us to put our trust in You more and more every day so we can pass with peace from moment to moment, day by day, and share this peace with others. Grant us to be this peace for others. Deliver us, Lord, from every evil and grant us peace in our day. Amen . . .

18
Vigil Prayer

"Keep watch because you do not know when the owner of the house will come back – whether in the evening, or at midnight, or when the rooster crows, or at dawn" (Mark 13:35).

Lord Jesus, our contemporary culture is not used to praying much in the first place. To keep vigil, to keep awake to pray at times when sleep is customary, is even more of a pressing challenge. Put within us a hunger for prayer — to pray at night, to wake ourselves up in the middle of the night to pray. Lord Jesus, conquer my fear of fatigue and human frailty and increase my faith and trust in Your divine power. Help me to be inspired and influenced by Your example of praying during and even through the night — to be in communion with You and the Father in the power of the Holy Spirit. May we be so moved by world events that if we rise in the middle of the night, even to go to the bathroom, we may willfully stay awake to pray even just a little bit.

Lord Jesus, I pray:

- ✞ for those this night trapped in temptation and sin . . . Lord, have mercy
- ✞ for those this night in immediate need of Your divine help . . . Lord, have mercy
- ✞ for those this night who need an increase of faith . . . Lord, have mercy
- ✞ for those who are dying and will die this night . . . Lord, have mercy
- ✞ for those who are runnin away from You this night . . . Lord, have mercy
- ✞ for those this night who hate themselves and find themselves unlovable . . . Lord, have mercy
- ✞ for those this night who hate others and find it hard to love . . . Lord, have mercy
- ✞ for those this night who are hurting themselves . . . Lord, have mercy

- for those this night who are hurting others... Lord, have mercy
- for those this night who are abusing drugs and alcohol... Lord, have mercy
- for those this night who are abusing their sexuality... Lord, have mercy
- for those who are victims of all kinds of abuse and for their abusers this night... Lord, have mercy
- for those this night who will rise tomorrow and have to face tragedy and difficulty... Lord, have mercy

19

Prayer 4 the World

"My prayer is not that you take them out of the world but that you protect them from the evil one. They are not of the world, even as I am not of it... As you sent me into the world, I have sent them into the world" (John 17:15-16, 18).

Lord Jesus, the Father loved the world so much He sent You — love itself. Love was the motivation for sending love, the real final solution to every problem in every culture and nation; love, the yearning and desire and destiny of every human heart and person in the world. The heart of the world hungers for love and the heart of the world is loved by the Father to such a degree that He sent You, and yet, Lord, this love is not loved. Save us, O Lord, from reducing this love to what we can manage and understand. Expand our hearts into the realm of the bigness of Your heart — the transcendent dimension of Your love, which is so simple and so available to everyone, everywhere. Protect me from the evil one. Father, may Your love for the world which moved You to send Your beloved Son so move me to be that love as You would have it . . . Amen . . .

20

Prayer Before Sleep

"I lie down and sleep; I wake again, because the LORD sustains me" (Psalm 3:5).

"I will lie down and sleep in peace, for you alone, O LORD, make me dwell in safety" (Psalm 4:8).

Lord, I thank You for this day. Did You get what You wanted from me today Lord? Please forgive all my sins this day and help me to learn from my mistakes and omissions — the things I may have forgotten to do, left undone, or didn't even notice. Help me to learn from Your love for me so I may be more loving and understanding of others tomorrow. May sleep refresh me tonight, so that I may truly be awake tomorrow — alert and attentive and responsive to all that You will have in store for me. Please bless all my family and friends, my enemies and those who have no one to pray for them — especially the Holy Souls in Purgatory. Please bless those who have no place to sleep tonight and accept my gratitude for my place of rest. Bless those hearts that are so heavy with trouble and pain that they will find it hard to sleep and those who will go to sleep with empty and hurting hearts and hungry stomachs. Bless them with peace. May Your presence in my life tonight give me the confidence to surrender my life to You as I surrender to sleep this night in peace. May Your mercy and light be with me always casting out all my fears with Your perfect love. Thank You, Lord . . . I love You, Lord . . . Thank You for everything . . . in Jesus' name . . . Amen . . .

III
Relationships

21

Heavenly Father

"The Father loves the Son and has placed everything in his hands" (John 3:35).

Heavenly Father, when I read the Gospels it becomes so clear that the relationship Jesus had with You during His earthly ministry was awesome. You placed everything in His hands. He had complete confidence in You, and that confidence was lived out in His complete obedience to Your will; this obedience energized Him in His prayer and ministry. Please help me today so that my relationship with You might be more like the relationship Jesus had with You. Help me to taste the depth of that communion with You, so that my life may reflect the confidence Jesus had with You, and so that my taste for obedience to seeking and doing Your Will might energize me and liberate me from all inordinate attachments to earthly relationships. As a result, may all my earthly relationships, including my use of things, be enriched by my renewed and deepened relationship with You. Father I adore You; help me to lay my life down before You so I can love You like Jesus does. Amen . . .

22

Jesus

"Greater love has no one than this, that he lay his life down for his friends. You are my friends if you do what I command. I no longer call you servants, because a servant does not know his master's business. Instead, I have called you friends, for everything that I learned from my Father I have made known to you" (John 15:13–15).

Jesus, it seems kinda weird to call You "friend." I guess I could get used to the idea. You're probably an awesome friend. Hopefully I could be a good friend to You, and that would help me to be a good friend to others. This is a tough thing today. Like most other relationships, friendships are ruled by selfishness — what is my friend gonna do for me. But, if I think about what You said a friend would do to show his love — lay down his life — I guess that's elevated friendship to another level. Help me not to be afraid of what You command and the ways You take us to higher levels of living and loving — the deep levels of giving ourselves. I guess that's what You do best: take us to another level and empower us to do that for one another. Jesus, help me to trust You and to rely on You and to call on You more and more, so I can learn how to be there for others as You are always there for me. Jesus, thank You for bein such an awesome friend. Please help me to be a good and true friend more and more like You. Thank You, Jesus . . .

23
The Holy Spirit

"The wind blows wherever it pleases. You hear its sound, but you cannot tell where it comes from or where it is going. So it is with everyone born of the Spirit" (John 3:8).

Holy Spirit, how awesome to know You, to have a relationship with You, to be born anew in You. All the saints must have had an awesome relationship with You. The freedom and joy of being likened to the wind, not to mention what power! All the stress worryin about direction in my life and what am I gonna do, where am I gonna go, who am I gonna be — no problem, so long as I trust in You and am born anew in You. O Holy Spirit, lead me, guide me; command me to know and do the Father's will like Jesus, so I can be filled with the power and joy of knowing You. Manifest Your fruits and gifts in me as You wish. Come, Holy Spirit, and breathe Your divine life in me. Purify me and energize me with the fire of Your love. Help me to believe that when I am weak I am strong and that I can do all things in You who strengthen me. I surrender all the obstacles and challenges in my life to You for You to transform them and use them for good, for my sanctification, and for the glorification of You with the Father and Jesus. Glory be to the Father, and to the Son, and to the Holy Spirit, as it was in the beginning, is now, and will be forever ... Amen ...

Mother Mary

"When Jesus saw his mother there, and the disciple whom he loved standing nearby, he said to his mother, 'Dear woman, here is your son,' and to the disciple, 'Here is your mother.' From that time on, this disciple took her into his home" (John 19:26–27).

Dear Mother Mary, be a mother to me now in the order of grace, as I welcome you into the home of my life. Restore to me the supernatural life that comes from your son, the supernatural life that you are so familiar with. Dearest mother of the impossible, pray for me and teach me to pray by instructing me in the mysterious ways of the Lord. Help not to be afraid of the things I feel and help me to transform my desires so that I may be pleasing to Jesus. May my love for Jesus be like yours, and may my doing of the Father's will be like your doing of the Father's will. Pray that my inner attitude may be more and more like yours — pure, obedient and receptive to the Holy Spirit — so that the will and word of God may be accomplished in me as it was in you. May I be faithful in carrying out your advice to do everything Jesus tells me to do. Pray for me now and always, especially at the hour of my death, and show always to me the blessed fruit of your womb, Jesus . . .

The Saints

"The saints tell us . . . they are sinners by their very nature, because of their human weakness, and thus they open themselves up to the Holy Spirit who begins to fill their hearts; they become converted, that is changed, changed interiorly, sublimated, made like God" (Pope John Paul II, Homily, June 20, 1993).

Lord Jesus, when I think of the saints I feel like "never happen to me." Please help me to understand that You experienced everything we do, yet You never sinned. Help me to be encouraged by the fact that the saints are not like You in that regard. The saints were tempted and fell into sin. They repented, confessed, and converted and needed You just as much as I do. But their inner life, their inner desire was so on fire that they continually opened themselves and kept themselves open to the Holy Spirit and all His fruits, gifts, and promptings. O saints of God, keep my heart focused on and open to the power of the Holy Spirit. When my weakness gets the best of me, show me, my celestial companions, how to yield to the Holy Spirit. Teach me to call on Him to work in my life every day. Help me, Jesus, to really get to know Your saints. May they become my good friends. May I learn from them, from their words, from their example; may I be influenced and inspired by every dimension of their life and their prayer for me, pushing me to keep my heart open to the Holy Spirit. May I rely on them to help me rely on You and the Holy Spirit to command me and captivate me, to know and do the Father's will with great abandon, surrender and joy. All you saints of God, pray for me . . .

26

My F.A.M.I.L.Y.

F.A.M.I.L.Y. is an acronym meaning:

F - Forget
A - About
M - Me
I - I
L - Love
Y - You

"He went down to Nazareth with them and was obedient to them. But his mother treasured all these things in her heart. And Jesus grew in wisdom and stature, and in favor with God and men"
(Luke 2:51–52).

Heavenly Father, from whom every family in heaven and on earth receives its name (see Hebrews 3:15), help me to know, love, and respect myself to such a degree that I can forget about myself and make a more perfect and complete gift of myself to my family — my blood family, my spiritual family, my extended family, the family of the Church, and the family of all peoples and cultures, the global universal family. As the source of all problems and pain for all families is rooted in the original disobedience and sin of our first parents, and as the remedy for all the problems and pain for all families is rooted in the awesome obedience of Jesus, Your Son, help me to know the fruit, freedom and joy of obedience. Help me to know, love, and respect myself in such an enlightened way that my greatest joy and fulfillment of self can be achieved through a generous and complete forgetting and giving of myself. May this self-gift be an expression and revelation of who I really am — a positive and life-giving contribution to love and the culture of solidarity. Help me to grow in wisdom and favor with You and all peoples ... Amen ...

27

Myself

"Whoever wants to save his life will lose it, but whoever loses his life for me will find it" (Matthew 16:25).

Lord Jesus, in the daily tensions, sufferings, and fatigue that are part of living in this fallen world, help me resist the temptation to selfishness which always lurks in the human heart. Deliver me from the desire to possess both things and persons and all the other negative effects, energies, and tendencies flowing from the consumer culture. Help me to find and save myself by overcoming the fear of losing myself. May the offering of my life to You be the losing of myself, resulting with the finding of myself — my real, true, and authentic self. Increase within me a burning passion for this endless journey; may it become more and more a delight for me, a source of the joy and peace You give to me — the joy and peace that are not of this world. Form and reform within me the values and virtues that sustain lasting joy and peace in this constantly changing world. Thank You, Jesus . . . Amen . . .

28

The Poor & Rich

"The parable of the rich man and Lazarus must always be present in our memory; it must form our conscience. Christ demands openness to our brothers and sisters in need – openness from the rich, the affluent, the economically advantaged; openness to the poor, the underdeveloped and the disadvantaged. Christ demands an openness that is more than benign attention [to show kindness with no significant effect], more than token actions or half-hearted efforts that leave the poor as destitute as before or even more so ... Nor can we remain indifferent when the rights of the human spirit are trampled upon, when violence is done to the human conscience in matters of truth, religion, and cultural creativity" (Pope John Paul II, Homily at Yankee Stadium, Bronx, New York, October 2, 1979).

Lord Jesus, social and economic poverty burden and kill too many people every day. Hunger, homelessness, and lack of education and basic human needs are just the tip of the iceberg. And yet, too many people have too much food and an overabundance of material goods and education. And still everybody's got to suffer. How strange and sad a reality that in the midst of so many cultures of choice and abundance, so many people have nothing and some people have too much, and yet both suffer from envy and jealousy. How mysterious the meaning of Your statements, "The poor you will always have with you" (Matthew 26:11), and, "It is hard for a rich man to enter into the kingdom of heaven" (Matthew 19:23). May the tension that exists between the poor and rich first of all be felt and embraced by my heart and not neglected and denied just because "I can't fix it." Please help me to somehow make a difference. In the most basic and important prayer we have from You, You taught us to pray for "our" daily bread, not "my" daily bread. May the lack of daily bread for so many of my brothers and sisters in my village, town, city, country, and our wounded world move my heart as the hungry crowds moved Your heart. And as You tended to the needs of the poor and hungry, help me to do something to tend to the needs of the poor and hungry — please, Lord Jesus, help me to do something. Most especially, please protect me from becoming bitter as a result of inequality and injustice. Make me bold in personal sacrifices for the good of others, and make me bold in calling others to the demands of generosity and justice, so that Lazarus can form and revive my conscience and the conscience of culture. Amen.

29

Community & Culture

"May God Almighty bless you and make you fruitful
and increase your numbers until you become a community of peoples" (Genesis 28:3).

Lord Jesus, help me to realize that community is the cultural remedy for the modern world. In light of all the differences between people on a personal, local, and global level, when I pray, "Our Father," please make what You meant by teaching me that prayer happen in my life. I know that means I'll have to change a lot of my inner attitudes and their outward expressions. I know that means I'll have to change how I see others as only useful to me — what they can do for me. Lord Jesus, help me make these changes. Help me to see others as opportunities for me to give of myself selflessly, in order to experience authentic self-realization and self-fulfillment. Renew Your Spirit within me and create within me a heart for others, a generous and loving heart that will find its greatest pleasure in giving. You told us, "It is more blessed to give than to receive" (Acts 20:35). Jesus, help me be a blessed builder and creator of community by responding to the Gospel impulse to give myself to others without expecting anything in return. Lord, have mercy . . . May the deep interior satisfaction, self-fulfillment, and joy of making a sincere gift of myself to others be the foundation for a new sense of community that every person so desperately longs for. Lord Jesus, help me to know how to make room for my brothers and sisters — to make them feel they belong, patiently bearing their burdens. Help me to resist the selfish temptations which constantly provoke me to be competitive — make me compassionate; help me resist the selfish temptations which make me focus on "my career" — help me to know my true vocation, to live in communion with You and all peoples . . . Amen . . .

30

Strangers

"I was a stranger and you invited me in" (Matthew 25:35).

Stranger: a person or thing that is unknown or with whom one is unacquainted; one who does not belong to or is kept from the activities of a group.

Lord Jesus, I know how bad it feels when I'm made to feel like I don't belong… even worse when I feel rejected… and worse still when I am actually rejected. Awaken within me a keen sense not only of Your mysterious presence in the stranger, but how they feel when they are not welcomed or made to feel that they don't belong. May this awareness be less from guilt and more from love. Heal me and help me conquer the fear of taking the risk to make others feel welcomed, especially in difficult situations — in my family, with my friends, at school, at work, in the street, in public and private places, with everyone everywhere. Help me to know the little things I can do that will make a big difference. May I be overjoyed at being ridiculed because of the initiative and risk I take in making others feel welcomed and that they belong. And if my efforts are rejected, give me the inner freedom and strength to be willing to take the risk again and again. May the reward of such awareness and action fill me with joy and sustain me with the freedom and power of love in this world and love forever in the world to come. Alleluia.

CHAPTER IV
Work

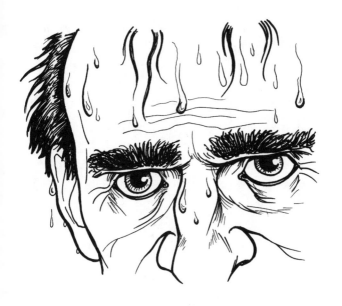

Divine Assistance

" I know you can do all things; no plan of yours can be thwarted" (Job 42:2).

"I can do everything through him who gives me strength" (Philippians 4:13).

Lord God, apart from You I can do nothing. Help me not to waste any more time trying to make it on my own without Your Help. With You all things are possible — especially the impossible. For this may You be the cause of my joy. May Your divine assistance move me to have such trust in You that no obstacle will be able to stop me from living life to the fullest, no matter the degree of difficulty or intensity of discouragement. Discouragement is one of the devil's most powerful weapons. May my reliance on Your divine assistance become my first and favorite option in overcoming all discouragement and adversity — may it be my safe shelter from all storms, my confidence in all moments of cowardice, my getting up from every knockdown, my peace as I peruse Your plan for my life. O God, come to my assistance; O Lord, make haste to help me as I pray with St. Teresa of Ávila, "O my God! Source of all mercy! I acknowledge Your sovereign power. While recalling the wasted years that are past, I believe that You, Lord, can in an instant turn this loss to gain. Miserable as I am, yet I firmly believe that You can do all things. Please restore to me the time lost, giving me Your grace, both now and in the future, that I may appear before You in 'wedding garments.'" Amen . . .

Humility & Zeal

"It is not good to have zeal without knowledge, nor to be hasty and miss the way" (Proverbs 19:2).

"The greatest among you will be your servant. For whoever exalts himself will be humbled, and whoever humbles himself will be exalted" (Matthew 23:11–12).

Lord Jesus, deliver me from the effects of pride and false humility. Set my heart on ideals and goals that are protected from these vices and the negative influences of modern culture which would have me aim at too little in life. May all disordered concerns for material gain and prosperity, resulting from the culture's "career" mentality, be subordinated to and integrated with a more vibrant sense of my life as vocation and mission through the teachings of Your Church. Set my heart on fire — make it burn with a love that serves and gives generously to all. Give me the heart of a servant. Renew within me the spirit of holy zeal; grant an increase of the spiritual authority in my life that comes from Your call for me to be a servant, with the freedom and joy that come along with it. Help me to humble myself today. Renew within me a striving for greatness in all that I do. May all that I am and the work that I do today be in the spirit of the Gospel and pleasing to You.

Reading & Study

"In reading this, then, you will be able to understand my insight into the mystery of Christ" (Ephesians 3:4).

"Devote yourself to the public reading of Scripture, to preaching and to teaching" (1 Timothy 4:13).

Holy Spirit, come into my heart and create a thirst for knowledge, a knowledge that is based on truth and the experience of love. Lead me ever more deeply into the mystery of Christ. Help me to quench this thirst through reading and studying with an increased spirit of prayer and devotion. Grant me the discipline necessary to make the time and to make the most productive use of time to read and study. Help me not to waste time. Make my heart sensitive and responsive to Your inspirations showing me what and when to read. May I always have something within my possession to read and study. Instill within me a hunger to memorize the word of God and some holy lines that will lead me into prayer in the depths of my heart. Lead me through the Scriptures so that, knowing what I read and studying what I know, I may be empowered to acknowledge the truth and be set free, delighting in the mystery of Your presence... Alleluia...

34
Leisure

"Be still, and know that I am God" (Psalm 46:10).

Lord, to be still in the midst of so much movement, to be focused in the midst of so many options and to be detached from all the concern and stress resulting from work — send Your Holy Spirit to help me. Grant me the spirit of leisure — freedom provided by the slowing down and cessation of activities, time free from work and duties. Help me to enjoy the present moment. Protect me from the spirit of idleness and laziness and instill within me stillness of heart and mind, so I can appreciate the beauty of all that is around me. May the anxious concern and stress about tomorrow be overcome by a simple trust in You right now. May the stilling of my heart, mind, body, and soul increase my knowledge of You, the knowledge that is acquired by experience.

Honesty

"Justice is driven back, and righteousness stands at a distance; truth has stumbled in the streets, honesty cannot enter. Truth is nowhere to be found, and who-ever shuns evil becomes a prey" (Isaiah 59:14–15).

Lord Jesus, it's so easy to de dishonest; it's too easy to be dishonest. In a culture that thrives on lookin good and being politically correct for the sake of gain, help me to be transformed by the renewal of my mind. Help me catch myself when I slip into the easy way of dishonesty through regular examination of conscience and confession. Send the Holy Spirit to help me live in such a way that I can be willing to strive to be more honest in my relations and dealings with others. Help my relationship with You, the Truth, to grow a little more every day, so that the freedom that comes from being in the truth will be more overwhelmingly delightful than the passing thrill of dishonest gain. In all the little things, Lord — lies of convenience, omissions, distortions, and denials of the truth — help me to grow and make progress every day. Amen . . .

Generosity & Justice

"When justice is done, it brings joy to the righteous but terror to evildoers" (Proverbs 21:15).

Lord Jesus, help me to do justice and be generous with a sense of what is due to You, to others, and to myself. Help me be generous with my time, talents and treasures. Not only to give when it's convenient and easy from my abundance, but help me to be generous and to give when it's really hard and when I don't have enough. To give with a sense of duty, the duty that flows from the order laid down by the Heavenly Father. Help me to feel the inequalities and injustices that prevail in our world in the lives of so many people that my heart may be in tune with the sentiments of Your heart, and that my life may be more of a reflection of You who are the justice of God. Help me to make a difference today with a generous spirit and attitude so my decisions can be an effective contribution to the renewal and reordering of a world desperately in need of real love and joy. Amen . . .

Vocation

"To you, O men, I call out; I raise my voice to all mankind. You who are simple, gain prudence; you who are foolish, gain understanding" (Proverbs 8:4–5).

"God did not call us to be impure, but to live a holy life. Therefore, he who rejects this instruction does not reject man but God, who gives you his Holy Spirit" (1 Thessalonians 4:7–8).

Heavenly Father, Your call reaches out to every person. You call every person to be holy because You are holy. Help me to hear Your call and to answer it in my life so that I may be holy. In the midst of so many distractions and attractions, may the force of Your voice be the never-failing source to lead me along the path You have marked out for me. May the force of Your voice be the never-failing power strengthening my weakness and weakening the strength of all that is contrary to Your call in my life — all the prominent and dominant cultural trends that compete for my attention to lessen and lower the high standard of holiness, the perfection of love. Keep me faithful to Your call, following wherever You would lead me, to do whatever You would have me do. Perfect love in my life and help me to be holy. Amen...

The Will of God

"Whoever does God's will is my brother and sister and mother" (Mark 3:35).

Lord Jesus, help me know and do God's will in my life every day. To know and to do God's will makes me a member of Your family. To help me live this way, You taught me to pray, "Our Father," asking for His will to be done "on earth as it is in heaven." To achieve this end of knowing and doing God's will, and to live as a member of Your F.A.M.I.L.Y. [Forget About Me I Love You], help me to forget about myself and express my love for You in the doing of the Father's will. By making a more complete gift of myself, transform all the incomplete areas of my life in the gradual, and more perfect knowing and doing of the Father's divine will every day. Amen . . .

The Kingdom of God

"The kingdom of God will be taken away from you and given to a people who will produce its fruit" (Matthew 21:43).

"I tell you the truth, anyone who will not receive the kingdom of God like a little child will never enter it" (Mark 10:15).

"No one who puts his hand to the plow and looks back is fit for service in the kingdom of God" (Luke 9:62).

"The kingdom of God is not a matter of eating and drinking, but of righteousness, peace and joy in the Holy Spirit, because anyone who serves Christ in this way is pleasing to God and approved by men" (Romans 14:17–18).

Lord Jesus, help me to produce the fruit of the kingdom in my life — righteousness, peace and joy in the Holy Spirit. May this be my greatest delight. Make my heart like that of a child, so that I may receive the kingdom like a child and enter it — not only after I die, but also now while I am alive. Help me to work for the building up of Your kingdom in this world. Help me not to hold back from the culture, so the life-giving message of the Gospel will not be silenced. Make me fit for service in the kingdom with a strengthening of my weak will with the power of Your Spirit. Renew me every day in my commitment to You and the building up of the kingdom. Help me not to look back at all the things that must be left behind, but rather keep my eyes firmly fixed on You, seeking first Your kingdom, so that all that I need in my life will be provided for by You in abundance. Thank You, Jesus . . .

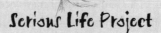

Serious Life Project

"Great are the works of the LORD; they are pondered by all who delight in them. Glorious and majestic are his deeds, and his righteousness endures forever" (Psalm 111:2–3).

"We pray this in order that you may live a life worthy of the Lord and may please him in every way; bearing fruit in every good work, growing in the knowledge of God, being strengthened with all power according to his glorious might so that you may have great endurance and patience, and joyfully giving thanks to the Father, who has qualified you to share in the inheritance of the saints in the kingdom of light" (Colossians 1:10–12).

Lord, great are all Your works. Help me to delight in them so that I may have a burning passion energizing me to commit to a serious life project. Whatever it may be, show me, Lord, and strengthen me for the task every day. Help me to do it in a way that is worthy of You, so that I may be pleasing to You in all that I do. Give me great patience and endurance to persevere in the tasks necessary to achieve something great with my life for Your glory and the good of all my brothers and sisters, and that deep fulfillment that comes only from You. Make me more aware of the inheritance of the saints you have given me to share in. Please bless the many people who are sad and have no sense of meaning and purpose in their lives. Shine Your light on them, and may Your beauty, ever ancient and ever new, touch them this day and open the eyes of their hearts. Amen . . .

CHAPTER V
Struggle

Trials & Hardships

"We must go through many hardships to enter the kingdom of God" (Acts 14:22).

"Consider it pure joy, my brothers, whenever you face trials of many kinds, because you know that the testing of your faith develops perseverance. Perseverance must finish its work so that you may be mature and complete, not lacking anything" (James 1:2–4).

"The Lord knows how to rescue godly men from trials" (2 Peter 2:9).

Lord, Your word makes it clear that there will be many trials and hardships along the path of following You. Lord, Your own life makes it clear that there will be many trials and hardships — You persevered through them all. All Your saints make it clear that there will be many trials and hardships — they persevered through them all. Why am I so surprised when I encounter trials and hardships in my following after You? Please help me not to be so surprised when trials and hardships come my way. Increase my faith in Your power to rescue me; bless me to consider it a pure joy when trials come! Because they come so often, just think how happy I will be! Do something for me on the inside. Pour into my heart Your Holy Spirit and make me yearn for the gifts that will condition me to go against the flow of all the cultural contradictions, flowing from the culture of death, that are in opposition to Your will. Help me to be mature and complete, lacking in nothing. With You as my provider, may I be used by You to build a new culture — the "civilization of love." Stay with me, Jesus . . . Amen . . .

Sorrow & Sadness

"The king asked me, 'Why does your face look so sad when you are not ill? This can be nothing but sadness of heart.' I was very much afraid" (Nehemiah 2:2).

"For with much wisdom comes much sorrow; the more knowledge, the more grief" (Ecclesiastes 1:18).

"My soul is overwhelmed with sorrow to the point of death" (Mark 14:34).

Lord, sometimes when I don't have a physical illness, there's something deep inside of me — heaviness of spirit, sorrow, sadness in my heart. Sometimes I don't even have to tell anybody because they can see it on my face. Sometimes I fight so hard to hide it. But that doesn't change a thing on the inside. Change my heart, O God, and make me ever new! Some of the stuff I know by experience brings me so much grief, but Lord, increase my knowledge of Your love by experience. Help me to experience the sorrow and sadness I feel in communion with Your sorrow — with the sadness and sorrow You felt — and what others feel, so that the hope of passing over to joy will sustain me. There is so much sadness in our culture filled with "worldly sorrow" that leads to death. Make my sorrow a "godly sorrow" that brings repentance, leads to salvation, and leaves no regret (see 2 Corinthians 7:8–11). No regrets... yes, Lord...

Fear & Rejection

"Have no fear of sudden disaster or of the ruin that overtakes the wicked, for the LORD will be your confidence and will keep your foot from being snared" (Proverbs 3:25–26).

"Fear of man will prove to be a snare, but whoever trusts in the LORD is kept safe" (Proverbs 29:25).

"Blessed are you when men hate you, when they exclude you and insult you and reject your name as evil, because of the Son on Man. Rejoice in that day and leap for joy, because great is your reward in heaven" (Luke 6:22–23).

Lord Jesus, the pain from being rejected and the fear of being rejected again is sometimes just too much. No matter what anybody says, it's just too much. Sometimes it's just plain old fear — fear of everything! Jesus, be my confidence and keep me from getting stuck in the traps of fear. Help all my fear of men — fear based in the human realm — to be overcome by trust in You to keep me safe. Help me to discover the power of the Gospel so that I might know myself as "blessed" when exclusion, rejection, and insult come my way because of my trusting in You. May the greatness of my reward in heaven inspire me to leap for joy in the face of the events that would cause me to be afraid. With You in my heart, and by my side, I have nothing to fear. Let Your words be my confidence, "Take courage! It is I. Don't be afraid" (Matthew 14:27). Thank You, Jesus . . . Amen . . .

Purity of Heart & Mouth

"He who loves a pure heart and whose speech is gracious will have the king for his friend" (Proverbs 22:11).

"Don't let anyone look down on you because you are young, but set an example for believers in speech, in life, in love, in faith and in purity" (1 Timothy 4:12).

"Blessed are the pure in heart, for they will see God" (Matthew 5:8).

ξ

Holy Spirit, come purify and sanctify my heart, mind, body and soul. Cleanse me from all the impure effects of the cultural corruption that is so widespread in the world — from all the habitual impurity that affects the way I see things and affects the way I speak. The mouth speaks from the abundance of the heart — purify my heart. Help me to receive the blessings that come to the pure of heart. Help me to see God in the midst of this fallen world. Help me to see the possibilities of a new way of being and seeing in the world so that my character can be formed and reformed according to image of God in all of its beauty and purity. By Your grace help me to be an example in speech, in life, in love, in faith, and in purity. Amen...

45
Sexual Purity

"Of this you can be sure: No immoral, impure or greedy person – such a man is an idolater – has any inheritance in the kingdom of Christ and of God" (Ephesians 5:5).

"Put to death, therefore, whatever belongs to your earthly nature: sexual immorality, impurity, lust, evil desires and greed, which is idolatry" (Colossians 3:5).

"The cowardly, the unbelieving, the vile, the murderers, the sexually immoral, those who practice magic arts, the idolaters and all liars – their place will be in the fiery lake of burning sulfur. This is the second death" (Revelation 21:8).

Lord Jesus, help me to respect and reverence my body and the bodies of others. Help me to accept the gift of sexuality and to protect it in a culture that has lost all respect for sexuality and the human body. Regardless of the culturally accepted practices and preferences of how people want to act on their sexuality, and the powerful, mind-molding effects of the media, help me to follow a different path — the path of sexual purity. Help me to acquire self-mastery. Help me to burn with a holy passion to make a more complete and pure gift of myself in all that I do and all that I am, so that my sexuality can be accepted as a gift and expressed in a way that is pleasing to you. Alleluia . . .

Anger & Violence

"A fool gives full vent to his anger, but a wise man keeps himself under control" (Proverbs 29:11).

"In your anger do not sin: do not let the sun go down while you are still angry, and do not give the devil a foothold" (Ephesians 4:26).

"You must rid yourselves of all such things as these: anger, rage, malice, slander, and filthy language from your lips" (Colossians 3:8).

ξ

Lord Jesus, the anger in my heart, the violent thoughts in my mind, the filthy language — all key elements of modern culture celebrated by the media — how can I get a grip on this? While waiting in line, on the road, at school, at work — even with friends and family, even on the telephone — so much anger! Help me, Jesus, to rid myself of anger, rage, malice, slander, and the filthy language. Help me to be quick to apologize and not let the sun go down on my wrath. Prevent me from being a fool and giving full vent to my anger. Bless me with the power of the Holy Spirit to keep me under control and to rely on Your divine assistance to be creative in dealing with anger with an abundance of patience. Thank You, Jesus . . .

47
Lies & the Truth

"A false witness will not go unpunished, and he who pours out lies will not go free" (Proverbs 19:5).

"He was a murderer from the beginning, not holding to the truth, for there is no truth in him. When he lies, he speaks his native language, for he is a liar and the father of lies" (John 8:44).

ord Jesus, You are the way, the truth, and the life. My relationship with You puts a duty and obligation on me to be honest and speak the truth. That means that I don't lie. Those little lies of convenience — I'd like to think that I'm honest, but, to be honest, I don't always tell the truth. Help me to overcome the fear of what would happen if I stopped telling those "little lies." Convict me that all lies come from the father of lies, and when I lie I speak his language. Help my "yes" to be "yes" and my "no" to be "no" — and any more than that comes from the evil one. I don't want to be associated with him, only You, Jesus. Bless me to experience the freedom that comes from telling the truth so that the delight of this freedom will be my strength in the face of the temptation to lie for the sake of convenience. Jesus, be my strength ... Amen ...

48

Envy & Jealousy

"A heart at peace gives life to the body, but envy rots the bones" (Proverbs 14:30).

"Do not let your heart envy sinners, but always be zealous for fear of the LORD" (Proverbs 23:17).

"Anger is cruel and fury overwhelming, but who can stand before jealousy?" (Proverbs 27:4).

Lord, sometimes the painful and resentful awareness of the advantages others have — the things they have that I don't have — causes me to be overwhelmed by envy and jealousy. Please help me with this, so that my heart can be at peace, and envy not rot the bones of my existence. Help me to be zealous for fear of You, so the wisdom that comes with the fear of the Lord can instruct me to move through the destructive forces of envy and jealousy. May I come through a better person and advance on the way of holiness. Help me to be grateful for the gifts that others have that I wish I had. Help me to delight in You, so that You will then grant the desires of my heart. I trust in Your word: "Delight yourself in the Lord and he will give you the desires of your heart" (Psalm 37:4). Lord, have mercy ... Amen ...

49

Trust & Surrender

"Trust in the LORD with all your heart and lean not on your own understanding; in all your ways acknowledge him, and he will make your paths straight" (Proverbs 3:5-6).

"Do not let your hearts be troubled. Trust in God; trust also in me" (John 14:1).

"May the God of hope fill you with all joy and peace as you trust in him, so that you may overflow with hope by the power of the Holy Spirit" (Romans 15:13).

eavenly Father, help me to yield to Your power and to give myself over to the influence and the inspiration of Your Holy Spirit. Help me in the struggle not to rely on my own understanding, so that I might trust in You to lead and guide me according to Your holy will like Jesus did. May my heart not be troubled in the midst of a troubled world because You are worthy of all my trust. As I surrender my life and my will to You, let Your peace be a shield that protects me from doubt and fear. Help me to make the prophet's words my own: "Surely God is my salvation; I will trust and not be afraid. The Lord, the Lord, is my strength and my song; he has become my salvation" (Isaiah 12:2).

Abusing the Body

"For we know that our old self was crucified with him so that the body of sin might be done away with, that we should no longer be slaves to sin" (Romans 6:6).

"Do not offer the parts of your body to sin, as instruments of wickedness, but rather offer yourselves to God, as those who have been brought from death to life; and offer the parts of your body to him as instruments of righteousness" (Romans 6:13).

"The body is not meant for sexual immorality, but for the Lord, and the Lord for the body" (1 Corinthians 6:13).

Lord, help me to change any abusive habits or patterns towards my body or the bodies of others — any violent physical means, through food or dress, drugs or alcohol, or any sexually immoral behavior, or sins of omission towards those in need. Help me to love, reverence, and respect my body and the bodies of others as temples of the Holy Spirit. Help me to give good care to my body through good eating and exercise habits, prayer, and rest, so I can use the members of my body as instruments of righteousness. Heal any memories of any kind of abuse done to me through another person or any other circumstances. Let Your divine light shine in the darkness of my heart and memory to bring peace and healing so I can restore the dignity and respect I owe to my body, as well as the bodies of others. Lord, help me to honor You with my body. Make me aware of the connection between my body and Your Mystical Body, the Church. Increase my reverence and respect for Your Body in the Eucharist, and Your presence in the bodies of all who suffer, most especially the sick, the hungry, and the poor. In You we are one body — Lord, have mercy . . .

CHAPTER

VI

Victory

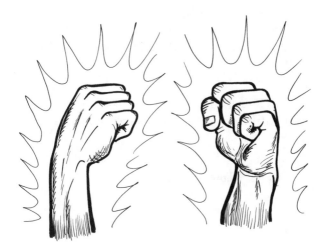

51
Willingness 2 Suffer

"He then began to teach them that the Son of Man must suffer many things and be rejected by the elders, chief priests and teachers of the law, and that he must be killed and after three days rise again" (Mark 8:31).

"We also rejoice in our sufferings because we know that suffering produces perseverance" (Romans 5:3).

"Christ suffered for you, leaving you an example, that you should follow in his steps" (1 Peter 2:21).

←

Lord Jesus, the necessity of suffering in this fallen world is unavoidable; to suffer willingly — by my own free choice, not reluctantly — is another story. Help my love for You increase to such a degree that I will be willing to suffer for You and with You. Your word makes it clear that You suffered out of love for me. May I embrace the cross daily, and suffer out of love for You and follow the example You left for me. May the Father's Love for You and Your love for the Father so inspire my love for You and for the Father that my heart will expand, make more room for the Holy Spirit, and be more willing to suffer. May this suffering produce perseverance in my life. Help me to find meaning and value in suffering in the midst of a culture that has no tolerance for suffering, finds no value whatsoever in suffering, and avoids it at all costs. Help me not to waste suffering . . . not to pass by opportunities to share in Your work as redeemer of the world. I love You, Jesus . . . Amen . . .

Healing & Holiness

"*Reckless words pierce like a sword, but the tongue of the wise brings healing*" (Proverbs 12:18).

"*Let us purify ourselves from everything that contaminates body and spirit, perfecting holiness out of reverence for God*" (2 Corinthians 7:1).

"*As God's chosen people, holy and dearly loved, clothe yourselves with compassion, kindness, humility, gentleness and patience*" (Colossians 3:12).

Lord Jesus, as a result of progress on the path to holiness, may reverence and respect for others increase in my life, along with compassion, kindness, humility, gentleness, and patience. May these expressions of love bring healing to the people I encounter every day. May the greatness of Your love cause me to be a wounded healer. Make me grow in wisdom, so the words I speak can bring healing to the culture so wounded from verbal pollution. Purify me in body and in spirit. Perfect my progress on the path of holiness. And may my surrender to Your perfecting process of sanctification be an expression of my reverence for You. I surrender to You all the areas of my life that are wounded by the effects of sin and are still in need of healing. Lord Jesus, I give You permission to have Your way with me . . . Amen . . .

Peace & Joy

"*There is deceit in the hearts of those who plot evil, but joy for those who promote peace*" (Proverbs 12:20).

"*Peace I leave with you; my peace I give you. I do not give to you as the world gives. Do not let your hearts be troubled and do not be afraid*" (John 14:27).

"*'Peace be with you!' After he said this, he showed them his hands and his side. The disciples were over-joyed when they saw the Lord*" (John 20:19–20).

ord Jesus, the world is desperately in need of peace. Hear my prayer for peace among the nations and the cultures of the world. You give peace as the world cannot give. Your Peace flows from a perfect love that casts out fear and calms trouble. My heart is in need of peace; the heart of the world is in need of peace. Open my heart and enable it to receive the peace You give, the peace that is beyond all understanding. Help me to promote peace and be a peacemaker, not fearing the trouble and conflict that prevents and disturbs peace. May the joy that comes to those who promote peace overflow from my heart and ease the pain of so many people in the world who long for peace, whose lives have been shattered, who are desperately waiting for the peace the world cannot give, the peace that comes from You. Make me a channel of Your peace. Thank You, Jesus . . . Amen . . .

54
Heaven & Earth

"Heaven and earth will pass away, but my words will never pass away" (Matthew 24:35).

"At the name of Jesus every knee should bow, in heaven and on earth and under the earth" (Philippians 2:10).

"In keeping with his promise we are looking forward to a new heaven and a new earth, the home of righteousness" (2 Peter 3:13).

⇐

Lord Jesus, the power of Your name, Your victory, and Your word is absolutely awesome and worthy of all my love, devotion, and respect — worthy of the reverence and respect of every creature in heaven and on earth. Heaven and earth will pass away, but Your word will never pass away. Help me be faithful to Your word. Help me to join the great chorus of praise with heaven and earth, the seas and all that move in them (see Psalm 69:34). Increase my awareness of the fullness of the awesomeness of Your victory, so that I may have a greater respect and reverence for the earth and the things of the earth. May I know and do the Father's will as You taught me to pray to do it — "on earth as it is in heaven." Let this knowledge condition me for deeper worship of You in the earthly and heavenly sanctuaries, providing me with the inner strength to persevere in looking forward, in the light of Your promise, for a new heaven and a new earth. Please keep me faithful in doing my part. Thank You, Jesus . . . Alleluia . . .

55
Fruit of the Spirit

"Those who live in accordance with the Spirit have their minds set on what the Spirit desires" (Romans 8:5).

"Live by the Spirit, and you will not gratify the desires of the sinful nature" (Galatians 5:16).

"The fruit of the Spirit is love, joy, peace, patience, kindness, goodness, faithfulness, gentleness and self-control" (Galatians 5:22–23).

←

Come, Holy Spirit! Come with Your power and help me to set my mind on what You desire. Come, Holy Spirit! Come into my heart that I might be more influenced and strengthened by Your presence not to gratify the desires of the sinful nature — sexual immorality, impurity, idolatry, and witchcraft, hatred, discord, jealousy, fits of rage, selfish ambition, dissentions, factions, envy, drunkenness, and orgies. Come, Holy Spirit! Come and fill my life with love, joy, peace, patience, kindness, goodness, faithfulness, gentleness, and self-control. I give You permission to make me more and more like Jesus. Come, Holy Spirit! Come that I might make You known and loved. Help me to bring to life the "culture of Pentecost," so the civilization of love can be built up and the friendly coexistence among peoples be increased. Come, Holy Spirit! Alleluia . . .

56

The Power of Prayer

"The Spirit helps us in our weakness. We do not know what we ought to pray for, but the Spirit himself intercedes for us with groans that words cannot express" (Romans 8:26).

"Be joyful in hope, patient in affliction, faithful in prayer" (Romans 12:12).

"I pray that out of his glorious riches he may strengthen you with power through his Spirit in your inner being" (Ephesians 3:16).

Holy Spirit, teach me how to pray. Help me to pray as I can, not as I can't. Help me in my weakness and intercede for me. Breathe in me, O Holy Spirit, and make me joyful in hope, patient in affliction, and faithful in prayer. Help me to know by experience the power of prayer in my life — the power of prayer for my family and friends, for all who sorrow and are without peace, for those weak in faith, for those with no hope and little love. May the cultures of the world be blessed and renewed through the power of prayer. May Your glorious riches be experienced in prayer so my life can give testimony to Your power, working through my weakness, in my inner being. Increase my devotion to prayer, that my love may abound more and more in knowledge and depth of insight, so that I may be able to discern what is best and may be pure and blameless until the day of Christ, filled with the fruit of righteousness that comes through Jesus Christ — to the glory and praise of God. Amen... (see Philippians 1:9–11).

My Weakness & God's Power

"*The weakness of God is stronger than man's strength ... God chose the weak things of the world to shame the strong*" (1 Corinthians 1:25, 27).

"*He said to me, 'My grace is sufficient for you, for my power is made perfect in weakness.' Therefore I will boast all the more gladly about my weaknesses, so that Christ's power may rest on me. That is why, for Christ's sake, I delight in weaknesses, in insults, in hardships, in persecutions, in difficulties. For when I am weak, then I am strong*" (2 Corinthians 12: 9–10).

"*He was crucified in weakness, yet he lives by God's power.*" (2 Corinthians 13:4).

←

Lord Jesus, I lack the strength to do the things I need to do in life, especially in my following You and keeping You first. I can't sustain the effort needed to keep my eyes fixed on You in the midst of a culture that overwhelms me with very powerful mind-molding images. My inner decision for You is too weak to withstand the onslaught of temptations and deceptions that have become part of life in modern culture. Failures from the past, things right now, and concern about the future make it hard for me to trust You. Help me to know by experience that you choose the weak things of the world to shame the strong — that You choose me, as weak as I am, to be filled with the power of Your truth and love in the heart of the world. May Your grace be enough for me so that Your power can be perfected in the weakness of my will and in all the areas of my life that suffer from weakness. Lord Jesus, increase my faith and bless me to know by experience that, because of my trust in You, when I am weak I am strong. Amen . . .

58

The Virtues & Temptations

"Watch and pray so that you will not fall into temptation. The spirit is willing, but the body is weak" (Mark 14:38).

"God is faithful; he will not let you be tempted beyond what you can bear. But when you are tempted, he will also provide a way out so that you can stand up under it" (1 Corinthians 10:13).

"As God's chosen people, holy and dearly loved, clothe yourselves with compassion, kindness, humility, gentleness and patience. Bear with each other and forgive whatever grievances you may have against one another. Forgive as the Lord forgave you. And over all these virtues put on love, which binds them all together in perfect unity" (Colossians 3:12–14).

←

Heavenly Father, Jesus was tempted, so please help me not to be surprised when temptations come my way. Sometimes it seems that life is a temptation! Send the Holy Spirit to help me watch and pray so I won't fall so easily into temptation. Father, I believe that You are faithful and that You won't let me be tempted beyond what I can bear; when temptations come, help me to trust in Your providing a way for me to stand up under the pressure of the temptation, no matter what it is! Help me realize that the virtues can't be practiced and lived without encountering and conquering their opposite vices — compassion and kindness overcoming indifference and meanness, humility overcoming pride, patience overcoming lack of patience, a forgiving heart overcoming an unforgiving heart, purity overcoming impurity, love overcoming hatred and lack of respect both for myself and all peoples! So with all the many different temptations that come every day and night, help me to become holy by trusting in You to provide a way for me to stand up under them and shine with the virtues! And when I fall, help me to remember, "Though a righteous man falls seven times, he rises again" (Proverbs 24:16). Alleluia.

Gratitude & Generosity

"The LORD is my strength and my shield; my heart trusts in him, and I am helped. My heart leaps for joy and I will give thanks to him in song" (Psalm 28:7).

"Give thanks to the LORD, call on his name; make known among the nations what he has done" (Psalm 105:1).

"You will be made rich in every way so that you can be generous on every occasion, and through us your generosity will result in thanksgiving to God. This service you perform is not only supplying the needs of God's people but is also overflowing in many expressions of thanks to God" (2 Corinthians 9:11–12).

←

O God, I wanna thank You with all my heart for being my shield, for being worthy of all my trust. Help my heart to feel the joy of being loved by You, so I can express my gratitude to You every day by making known to others generous expressions of Your goodness to me. Help me penetrate the contemporary culture, so conditioned by greed and selfishness, with the good news of Your love and goodness expressed through generous and selfless deeds. Enrich me in every way, so I can be generous on every occasion, so that my generosity will result in an awesome chorus of thanksgiving to You. "To you, O LORD, I called . . . 'Hear, O LORD, and be merciful to me; O LORD, be my help.' You turned my wailing into dancing; you removed my sackcloth and clothed me with joy, that my heart may sing to you and not be silent. O LORD my God, I will give you thanks forever" (Psalm 30:8–12).

Luminous Countenance

"The path of the righteous is like the first gleam of dawn, shining ever brighter till the full light of day" (Proverbs 4:18).

"You are the light of the world. A city on a hill cannot be hidden. Neither do people light a lamp and put it under a bowl. Instead they put it on its stand, and it gives light to everyone in the house. In the same way, let your light shine before men, that they may see your good deeds and praise your Father in heaven" (Matthew 5:14–16).

"For you were once darkness, but now you are light in the Lord. Live as children of light (for the fruit of the light consists in all goodness, righteousness and truth) and find out what pleases the Lord" (Ephesians 5:8–10).

⬅

Lord Jesus, You came into the world as light — the light of the world — so that those who believe in You should not remain in darkness. Help me to shine like the stars in the midst of the darkness of the twisted and depraved culture of death — a culture that loves darkness rather than light because its deeds are evil, a culture that does not want to come into the light for fear its deeds will be exposed. Empower me to be true to my vocation as the light of the world. Help me to be like a city on a hill, not hidden; make me like a bright lamp shining, giving light to all around me. Lead me along the luminous path of doing good deeds, so that others may see these deeds and give praise to our Father in heaven. Each day, Lord, let me live as a child of the light and bear abundant fruit of the light — goodness, righteousness, and truth. May I know what pleases You and may I do it every day with great love and fidelity. Make the light shine in my heart and my eyes, on my face, and through all that I am and all that I do. Thank You, Jesus . . . Amen . . .

CHAPTER VII
Mystery

Me

"If anyone is in Christ, he is a new creation; the old has gone, the new has come!" (2 Corinthians 5:17).

"God raised us up with Christ and seated us with him in the heavenly realms in Christ Jesus. In order that in the coming ages he might show the incomparable riches of his grace, expressed in his kindness to us in Christ Jesus" (Ephesians 2:6–7).

"Since, then, you have been raised with Christ, set your hearts on things above, where Christ is seated at the right hand of God" (Colossians 3:1).

Lord Jesus, may the mystery of who You are so captivate my heart and mind that the mystery of who I am, and who You call me to be, will form, reform, and define my character. Help me to have a greater realization of myself as a new creation in You. — to experience what it means, in my daily life, to be seated with You in the heavenly realms as I experience life on earth, to go against the flow of the negative and destructive energy of the culture with the positive and constructive light of Your kingdom. As I try to live my life in the heart of the Church and in the heart of the world, make me know by experience, now, what it means to be raised up with You. Help me to set my heart on things above, where You are seated at the right hand of God the Father, so that the quality of my living and the character of who I am will give glory to You and be beneficial to others. Thank You, Jesus . . . Alleluia . . .

Others

"*A generous man will prosper; he who refreshes others will himself be refreshed*" (Proverbs 11:25).

"*In the same way you judge others, you will be judged, and with the measure you use, it will be measured to you . . . In everything, do to others what you would have them do to you*" (Matthew 7:2, 12).

"*I tell you the truth, whatever you did for one of the least of these brothers of mine, you did for me*" (Matthew 25:40).

ट

Lord Jesus, make me sensitive to the mystery of Your presence in others. Help me to be aware of the needs of others and to respond to those needs in the best way I can; give me a generous heart that will empower me to bring others refreshment through generous and loving service, through giving of myself. Let the measure I use towards others be the measure used towards me! Help me to do everything to others in the same way I would want them to do it to me! Most especially, make me always responsive to the mystery of Your presence in the poor, in those who suffer from sickness, from being in prison, from lack of food, shelter and clothing, in the lonely and rejected — in those who suffer in any way. May the mystery of You thirsting for souls, and You thirsting in souls, be quenched by my love for You. I love You, Jesus . . .

The Word of God

"Every word of God is flawless; he is a shield to those who take refuge in him" (Proverbs 30:5).

""The grass withers and the flowers fall, but the word of our God stands forever" (Isaiah 40:8).

"The word of God is living and active. Sharper than any double-edged sword, it penetrates even to dividing soul and spirit, joints and marrow; it judges the thoughts and attitudes of the heart" (Hebrews 4:12).

٢

Lord, Your word is awesome! Help me to love Your word. Help me to read the Bible — to make time to read the Bible — and learn how to take refuge in You, so You can be my protection, my shield. May I be less concerned about what I understand or don't understand, and more concerned about You speaking to me when I read the sacred Scriptures. May Your word cut away any fear and doubt concerning the mystery of Your voice in the Scriptures and the events of my life; may Your word penetrate deep into my being, judging the thoughts and attitudes of my heart, helping me to change the bad ones and grow stronger in the good ones. Fascinate my mind and heart with the beauty of Your mystery. Attune my mind to the sound of Your voice so I may follow You. All the beautiful things of creation will eventually fade away, but Your word stands forever. Thank You for the gift and challenge of Your word. Amen . . .

Holy Mass

"I am the living bread that came down from heaven. If anyone eats of this bread, he will live forever. This bread is my flesh, which I will give for the life of the world" (John 6:51).

"For I received from the Lord what I also passed on to you: The Lord Jesus, on the night he was betrayed, took bread, and when he had given thanks, he broke it and said, 'This is my body, which is for you; do this in remembrance of me.' In the same way, after supper he took the cup, saying, 'This cup is the new covenant in my blood; do this, whenever you drink it, in remembrance of me'" (1 Corinthians 11:23–25).

"Whoever eats the bread or drinks the cup of the Lord in an unworthy manner will be guilty of sinning against the body and blood of the Lord" (1 Corinthians 11:27).

Lord Jesus, the mystery of all mysteries is You taking on flesh in the womb of Your Mother Mary, combined with Your real presence in the sacred mysteries manifested at the holy sacrifice of the Mass. The bread You give is Your flesh for the life of the world. May the power of the sacrifice of the Mass be welcomed by my heart, mind, body, and soul — may it be welcomed by my whole life to energize and sustain me in living life to the fullest, preparing me for eternal life by strengthening me to build up the culture of life. Help me to repent and prepare for every Mass in a worthy fashion; only say the word and I shall be healed, because I am not worthy — You alone are worthy. And whenever I partake of holy Communion at Mass in an unworthy manner and sin against Your Body and Blood, help me make a good confession. May all external conditions of boredom, or even high energy and enthusiasm or whatever, never prevent me from experiencing the power and delight that comes to us at every celebration of holy Mass. By participating more fully in this most awesome mystery, help me to learn from You the joy of giving myself completely to You and to others, as You give Yourself completely to me and to the world. Thank You, Jesus . . .

65

The Blessed Sacrament

"Here is the bread that comes down from heaven, which a man may eat and not die. I am the living bread that came down from heaven. If anyone eats of this bread, he will live forever. This bread is my flesh, which I will give for the life of the world" (John 6:50–51).

"Christ did this to bring us to a closer bond of friendship, and to signify His Love towards us, giving Himself to those who desire Him, but also to handle Him, to eat Him, to embrace Him with the fullness of their whole heart. Therefore, as lions breathing fire do we depart from the table rendered objects of terror to the devil" (St. John Chrysostom, Homilies on the Gospel According to St. John, #46).

"In the Eucharist we have Jesus, we have his redemptive sacrifice, we have his resurrection, we have the gift of the Holy Spirit, we have adoration, obedience and love of the Father. Were we to disregard the Eucharist, how could we overcome our own deficiency?" (Pope John Paul II, Ecclesia de Eucharistia, #60).

?

ord Jesus, the mystery of Your real presence in the Blessed Sacrament is the medicine to restore and sustain unity of life — unity of life in this world and in the world to come. Protect me from one of the most serious errors on the modern age, the separation of the faith I profess and the life that I live, and the separation of the Gospel from culture. Make the simplicity and complexity of this great sacrament cause me to be an authentic adorer in spirit and truth, so that my life might become more simple, transforming all the complexities and challenges in my life into occasions for growth and an increase of joy and peace — a joy and peace that the world cannot give but so desperately needs. Make my preparation, reception, and adoration of this great sacrament the effective means to deepen my communion with You through a real spirituality of communion. May this communion be so real that my encounter with, experience of and contribution to all peoples and events will be experienced through You, with You and in You, in the unity of the Holy Spirit, that I might become love in the heart of the Church and in the heart of the world, giving all glory and honor to the Father now and forever ... Amen ...

66

The Church

"In the church God has appointed first of all apostles, second prophets, third teachers, then workers of miracles, also those having gifts of healing, those able to help others, those with gifts of administration, and those speaking in different kinds of tongues" (1 Corinthians 12:28).

"Try to excel in gifts that build up the church" (1 Corinthians 14:12).

"God placed all things under his feet and appointed him to be head over everything for the church, which is his body, the fullness of him who fills everything in every way" (Ephesians 1:22–23).

?

Lord Jesus, help me to love You and to love the Church. Help me not only to acknowledge and respect all the different gifts of service in the Church, but please also help me to make a generous contribution of my gifts to the service of the Church to build up the Church. Enliven within me a real sense of communion — communion of You with me, me with You, me with the Church, and the Church with You, all peoples, and all things. Your Mystical Body, the Church, represents You who are the fullness of all things, filling everything in every way. May my love, devotion, reverence, and respect for You, Your Church, and all peoples and all things grow and increase every day to expand my heart for more love. Bless the Pope, the rock on which You build Your Church, which the gates of hell shall not prevail against. Bless the bishops, priests, deacons, religious, and all the lay faithful who serve the Church; bless all those who find it hard to love the Church; bless all those who have been hurt and disappointed by the Church; bless all believers and nonbelievers. Jesus, help me to love You and to love Your Church and all peoples a little bit more every day. Alleluia . . .

The Street

"Wisdom calls aloud in the street, she raises her voice in the public squares; at the head of the noisy streets she cries out, in the gateways she makes her speech" (Proverbs 1:20–21).

"Go to the street corners and invite to the banquet anyone you find" (Matthew 22:9).

"Destructive forces are at work in the city; threats and lies never leave its streets" (Psalm 55:11).

؟

O God, every day as I make my way through the street, protect me from the visible and invisible destructive forces that are at work. Help me to hear the voice of wisdom calling out, not just in the quiet places, but also in the noisy public places in the street. Make me a courageous witness of Your presence and Your desire to invite all peoples to Your banquet, to Your kingdom. May my actions speak louder than my words, and may my words, when necessary, make it clear that I am loved. May this love, Your love for me and all people, Your divine love, be seen, heard, tasted, and felt through my love, through the way I conduct and express myself, through the way I speak and dress, through respect and kindness towards others, and through all the virtues of the civilization of love shining in the darkness of all the vices of the culture of death. May the suffering and sadness of the masses in the streets of the world and my neighborhood be lessened and blessed with peace and joy, as I make my way every day . . . Amen . . .

68

The Rosary

"From now on all generations will call me blessed, for the Mighty One has done great things for me – holy is his name" (Luke 1:48–49).

"Mary treasured up all these things and pondered them in her heart" (Luke 2:19).

"Do whatever he tells you" (John 2:5).

?

Mother Mary, God has done great things for you. You are blessed among all women of all generations. Make the chain of events of my life be evermore conformed to and renewed by the events of the life of your son, Jesus — the events you treasured and pondered continuously in your heart. Help me to be a good student in your school of the Rosary. By meditating on the mysteries of the Rosary may I be strengthened to do whatever Jesus tells me. Teach me the meaning and value of suffering, and be the cause of my joy by leading me and keeping me close to Jesus. May the light of the luminous mysteries energize me to walk faithfully on the narrow path that leads to glory. Through your loving and powerful intercession, may my meditation and contemplation of these holy mysteries inspire me to imitate what they contain and obtain what they promise. Amen . . .

Communion

"Remain in me, and I will remain in you. No branch can bear fruit by itself; it must remain in the vine. Neither can you bear fruit unless you remain in me" (John 15:4).

"As the Father has loved me, so have I loved you. Now remain in my love" (John 15:9).

"Just as each of us has one body with many members, and these members do not all have the same function, so in Christ we who are many form one body, and each member belongs to all the others" (Romans 12:4–5).

?

Dear Jesus, may Your perfect love cast out the fear of having an intimate relationship with You, the fear of You being close to me, the fear of others being close to me — the fear of me being close to You and to others in my life. Strengthen me to face this great challenge, the challenge of having a close relationship with You and with others in the midst of a culture that thrives on selfishness and takes advantage of close relationships for personal gain. Teach me more and more to make a sincere gift of myself as the means for achieving and sustaining close relationships. Help me to see Your face shining in the faces of those around me. Help me to think of others as those who are a part of me, and a part of You. Open my eyes to see what is positive in others, to acknowledge their gifts as coming from the Father, and to welcome them as gifts for me! Expand my heart with the love that makes room for others and desires to help carry their burdens. Bless my heart to rejoice walking on this path of living a spirituality of communion. Thank You, Jesus ... Amen ...

Heaven

"Repent for the kingdom of heaven is near" (Matthew 4:17).

"When you stand praying, if you hold anything against anyone, forgive him, so that your Father in heaven may forgive you your sins" (Mark 11:25).

"Love your enemies and pray for those who persecute you, that you may be sons of your Father in heaven. He causes his sun to rise on the evil and the good, and sends rain on the righteous and the unrighteous" (Matthew 5:44–45).

ς

Heavenly Father, You have loved us so completely in Christ You have made us citizens of heaven. Please help me to live that way, to live as a citizen of heaven in the midst of the world, as a pilgrim and stranger. May my daily repentance for all wrongdoing and lack of love empower me to know and do Your will on earth as it is in heaven, just as Jesus taught me to pray. Help me to forgive and let go of whatever I hold against those who have done me wrong so that the joy and peace of heaven might shine through me. Forgive me my sins, Father, as I forgive those who sin against me. Assist me with Your divine providence, that I might rely on You to love my enemies and pray for those who persecute me, those who don't understand me, those who don't accept me, those who reject me, and those who have hurt me and let me down. Father, You are so good You cause Your sun and rain to fall on the good and bad, the righteous and the unrighteous. May this tremendous and outrageous love that reigns in heaven reign in my heart today and every day . . . Alleluia . . . Amen . . .

CHAPTER VIII
Faith

Not By Sight

"Faith is being sure of what we hope for and certain of what we do not see" (Hebrews 11:1).

"We live by faith not by sight" (2 Corinthians 5:7).

"The testing of your faith develops perseverance. Perseverance must finish its work so that you may be mature and complete, not lacking anything" (James 1:3–4).

"Faith by itself, if it is not accompanied by action, is dead" (James 2:17).

Lord Jesus, give me the gift of faith. Even of it's the size of a mustard seed, instill deep with in me the gift of faith, because even with this small amount of faith I can move mountains. Send the Holy Spirit to stir up that faith within me for me to practice it, to protect it, to learn to love it, and to read and study about it. Train me in the way of faith making me sure of what I hope for and certain about what I do not see. Help me to live by faith, not by sight. Establish me in the obedience that comes from faith, a living faith that is always accompanied by action and good works. Lord Jesus, when my faith is tested, find me ready to accept and embrace it so that perseverance may develop and become ever stronger in my life. May this perseverance make me mature and complete, lacking in nothing, that I might be pleasing to You and useful in helping my brothers and sisters and all peoples along the way. Amen . . .

72
Not By Might

"When your herds and flocks grow large and your silver and gold increase and all you have is multiplied, then your heart will become proud and you will forget the LORD your God, who brought you out of Egypt, out of the land of slavery" (Deuteronomy 8:13–14).

"The mighty man will became tinder and his work a spark; both will burn together, with no one to quench the fire . . . The LORD Almighty has a day in store for all the proud and lofty, for all that is exalted (and they will be humbled)" (Isaiah 1:31; 2:12).

"'Not by might nor by power, but by my Spirit,' says the LORD Almighty" (Zechariah 4:6).

Heavenly Father, protect me from the destructive pleasure of power. Send the necessary graces to protect my heart from being corrupted by abusing power, the power that comes from every good gift You give in heart, mind, body, and soul. Prevent my heart from becoming proud, for You "hate pride and arrogance" (Proverbs 8:13). May I never forget — in fact help me always — to remember that every good thing that I have or do, every good thing that every person has or does, every good thing that exists or is accomplished in the world is Your gift. May all people who have been seduced by mighty and arrogant attitudes welcome Your mercy for a change of heart because You will not tolerate those attitudes and ultimately all that has been accomplished by them will be destroyed. You have a day in store for all the proud and mighty, — for all that are puffed up, selfish, and exalted — all will be humbled. Help me to feel deep in my bones and to know with all my heart, mind, strength, and soul that it is not by might nor by power, but by Your Spirit. May I live that way for Your glory and the well-being and salvation of myself and all the world . . . Amen . . .

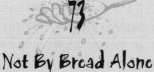

73

Not By Bread Alone

"Man does not live on bread alone but on every word that comes from the mouth of the LORD" (Deuteronomy 8:3).

"I have not departed from the commands of his lips; I have treasured the words of his mouth more than my daily bread" (Job 23:12).

"Now he who supplies seed to the sower and bread for food will also supply and increase your store of seed and will enlarge the harvest of your righteousness" (2 Corinthians 9:10).

Lord Jesus, when You were tempted in the desert You fought off the temptations of the devil, overcoming him by reminding him that man does not live on bread alone but on every word that comes from the mouth of God. Renew my spirit and adjust my appetites. Lord Jesus, so many times I have different appetites, so many different instinctive desires and inner cravings. Help me to yield to the commands of Your Gospel and Your Church; help me to treasure these teachings more than my daily bread. Increase my trust in the Heavenly Father so that my relying on His divine providence for daily bread, for all that I need, will sustain me when the influence and attractions of the culture of death try to convince me to depart from the path of obedience. As the Father provides for the needs of the body, see to it that He also provides in abundance for the needs of the soul and enlarges the harvest of holiness and righteousness, empowering me to build up the culture of life and the civilization of love. Thank You, Jesus . . . Amen . . .

The Future

"'I know the plans I have for you,' declares the LORD, 'plans to prosper you and not to harm you, plans to give you hope and a future'" (Jeremiah 29:11).

"Consider the blameless, observe the upright; there is a future for the man of peace. But all sinners will be destroyed; the future of the wicked will be cut off" (Psalm 37:37–38).

"Know also that wisdom is sweet to your soul; if you find it, there is a future hope for you, and your hope will not be cut off" (Proverbs 24:14).

Heavenly Father, I believe You know the plans You have for me, plans for me to prosper, plans to give me hope and a future. Help me to be blameless and upright in trusting You and Your plan for me in the midst of a culture that is fascinated with and dominated by information regarding progress, development, results, and knowledge of what is going to happen. Bless me with the peace that is beyond all understanding — peace beyond any predictions about my future, my vocation, my career, the health and well-being of me, my family or friends, and my anxious wondering about anything in the midst of such intense cultural curiosity! Please bless those who are so stressed out about the future that they sin and consult palm readers and psychics and faithfully read horoscopes. Grant them the graces of repentance, conversion, confession, and trust in You. Please send the Holy Spirit to convict them in their hearts that these activities are wicked and that the future of the wicked will be cut off. Dispose my soul to the sweetness of wisdom. Help me to seek and find wisdom, so I can be secure and free regarding my future, confident that my hope will not be cut off. Alleluia . . .

75

The Past

"Whatever is has already been, and what will be has been before; and God will call the past to account" (Ecclesiastes 3:15).

"Forget the former things; do not dwell on the past. See, I am doing a new thing! Now it springs up; do you not perceive it? I am making a way in the desert and streams in the wasteland" (Isaiah 43:18–19).

"Everything that was written in the past was written to teach us, so that through endurance and the encouragement of the Scriptures we might have hope" (Romans 15:4).

Lord Jesus, release the grip the past has on me, whether it be the things I have done, the things I haven't done, the things that were done to me, or the effect of the good things I have been deprived of. Direct my steps in light of the truth that You will call the past to account. Empower me with Your divine mercy to do what needs to be done so I can be healed and forget the things of the past. Open the eyes of my heart to see You do a new thing with me and with all people who suffer so much from bein stuck in the past. Jesus, help me to learn from the Scriptures that what was written in the past was written to teach me now how to endure, and to give me the inner strength to inspire me with courage, that I might have hope and share that hope with others ... Thank You, Jesus ... Amen ...

The Present

"Do not say to your neighbor, 'come back later; I'll give it tomorrow' – when you now have it with you" (Proverbs 3:28).

"I tell you the truth, today you will be with me in paradise" (Luke 23:43).

"Seek first his kingdom and his righteousness, and all these things will be given to you as well. Therefore do not worry about tomorrow, for tomorrow will worry about itself. Each day has enough trouble of its own" (Matthew 6:33–34).

Lord Jesus, the culture of abundance, while at times a blessing, tends to promote waste; wasting food, wasting money, wasting resources — water, electricity, the air, the earth — wasting time, wasting opportunities for love and truth, and therefore wasting the present moment. Please protect me from the negative impact of the culture of abundance, which is dominated by selfishness and greed. Help me to learn from my mistakes and from the mistakes of others, that I might make the most of the present moment by making a sincere gift of myself, and build up the culture of life. Help me to do what I can do and be all that I can be for my neighbor now! Prevent me from putting off till tomorrow what I can do today. Help me to be like the good thief who made the most of the present moment by turning to You and secured paradise when You assured him, "Today you will be with me in paradise" (Luke 23:43). Lord Jesus, transform me by increasing my faith and renewing my mind, that I might seek first the kingdom of God and His righteousness. Let the peace and serenity that comes from this belief relieve all the concern and anxiety resulting from the pressing needs in my life, in the Church, and in the world this day. Help me to live the faith of the Gospel and not worry about tomorrow, for tomorrow will worry about itself. Like You said, "Each day has enough trouble of its own" (Matthew 6:34). Thank You, Jesus, thank You, Jesus, thank You, Jesus . . . Amen . . .

The Promise

"My comfort in my suffering is this: Your promise preserves my life . . . May Your unfailing love be my comfort, according to your promise to your servant" (Psalm 119:50, 76).

"He redeemed us in order that the blessing given to Abraham might come to the Gentiles through Christ Jesus, so that by faith we might receive the promise of the Spirit" (Galatians 3:14).

"The Lord is not slow in keeping his promise, as some understand slowness. He is patient with you, not wanting anyone to perish, but everyone to come to repentance. But the day of the Lord will come like a thief. The heavens will disappear with a roar; the elements will be destroyed by fire, and the earth and everything in it will be laid bare. Since everything will be destroyed in this way, what kind of people ought you to be? You ought to live holy and godly lives as you look forward to the day of God and its coming. That day will bring about the destruction of the heavens by fire, and the elements will melt in the heat. But in keeping with his promise we are looking *forward to a new heaven and a new earth, the home of righteousness. So then, dear friends since you are looking forward to this, make every effort to be found spotless, blameless and at peace with him" (2 Peter 3:9–14).*

Lord, the pain and suffering resulting from the disappointment of broken promises are overwhelming. Let my comfort in my suffering come from the promise of Your unfailing love. Let the promise of the Holy Spirit to be with me and strengthen me in my weakness help me see the big picture and keep in view that You are not slow in keeping Your promise, but rather it's Your patience and love, Your desire for no one to perish, Your desire for all to come to repentance and knowledge of the truth, Your desire for all people to know themselves as loved. All the beauty of the created world will one day come to an end. Renew my spirit in light of Your promise for a new heaven and a new earth. Knowing that life as we see it now will one day come quickly to an end, help me not to be afraid, but highly motivated and energized to live a holy and godly life. Help me to conduct myself in this world with a vision of faith, looking forward to the fulfillment of Your divine will on earth as it is in heaven — the fullness of love. By the power of

Your unfailing love, assist me in making every effort to be found spotless and blameless and at peace with You, at peace with myself and at peace with all people. Lord, have mercy . . . Amen . . .

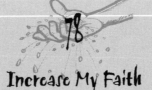

Increase My Faith

"The apostles said to the Lord, 'Increase our faith!' He replied, 'If you have faith as small as a mustard seed, you can say to this mulberry tree, "Be uprooted and planted in the sea," and it will obey you'" (Luke 17:5–6).

"'If you can do anything, take pity on us and help us.' 'If you can?' said Jesus. 'Everything is possible for him who believes.' Immediately the boy's father exclaimed, 'I do believe, help me overcome my unbelief!'" (Mark 9:22–24).

"When he had gone indoors, the blind men came to him, and he asked them, 'Do you believe that I am able to do this?' 'Yes Lord,' they replied. The he touched their eyes and said, 'According to your faith will it be done to you'; and their sight was restored" (Matthew 9:28–30).

Lord Jesus, increase my faith. Give me that bold inner attitude that will attempt to uproot a mulberry tree and have it planted in the sea. Help me make this teaching of Yours, Jesus, real in my life now, just as You intended it to be. Give me the faith and inner confidence to move mountains, mountains of self-hatred, doubt, despair, the effects of sin, lack of forgiveness, injustice, indifference to You and to others, hurts, old resentments and wounds, bad habits and addictions, greed, lust, and everything that keeps my heart from being free and full of the light of truth, love, and joy. Jesus, You said everything is possible to those who believe. That means nothing is impossible to those who believe. Help me acquire a taste for the impossible with an increase of faith. Increase my faith, Lord, and help me overcome my unbelief, so that according to my faith, increased by You, it will be done to me as I believe . . . Alleluia . . . Thank You, Jesus . . .

79

The Dark Night of Faith

"Your wrath has swept over me; your terrors have destroyed me. All day long they surround me like a flood; they have completely engulfed me. You have taken my companions and loved ones from me; the darkness is my closest friend" (Psalm 88:16–18).

"You, O LORD, keep my lamp burning; my God turns my darkness into light" (Psalm 18: 28).

"Even in the darkness light dawns for the upright, for the gracious and compassionate and righteous man" (Psalm 112:4).

"If I say, 'Surely the darkness will hide me and the light become night around me,' even the darkness will not be dark to you; the night will shine like the day, for darkness is as light to you" (Psalm 139:11–12).

Lord Jesus, sometimes I feel that my closest friend is darkness. Some days it's just too much. Please keep the light of faith burning in my heart; enlighten the darkness of my heart and turn my darkness into light. Help me to know by faith that even the darkness is not dark to You. Help me to see like You see, because with You the night shines like the day, for darkness is light to You. Lord Jesus, You experienced the dark night of faith when You felt forsaken by the Father. Help me to connect my feelings when I suffer with how You felt when You suffered, so that, like You, I will be able to pray in the most difficult moments and in the darkest times, "Father...not my will, but yours be done" (Luke 22:42). Jesus, stay with me always. Amen...

80

Faith and Reason

"Trust in the LORD with all your heart and lean not on your own understanding; in all your ways acknowledge him, and he will make your paths straight" (Proverbs 3:5–6).

"Whoever gives heed to instruction prospers, and blessed is he who trusts in the LORD" (Proverbs 16:20).

"Faith and reason are like two wings on which the human spirit rises to contemplation of truth; and God has placed in the human heart a desire to know truth – in a word, to know himself – so that, by knowing and loving God, men and women may come to the fullness of truth about themselves" (Pope John Paul II, Fides et Ratio).

Lord, help me to trust in You with all my heart, and not to rely on my own understanding. Let my use of reason, combined with faith, be like wings to lift me up to the contemplation of truth. Help me to grow and prosper in my life by paying attention to instruction from You and others who are wise in the ways of truth. May my faith and reason help me to know You. In coming to really know You and Your love for me and for all people, may I come to the fullness of truth about myself combined with the joy that comes from making an authentic gift of myself more and more every day. Amen. Alleluia . . .

CHAPTER
IX
Hope

The Goal — Heaven

"*I have come down from heaven not to do my own will but to do the will of him who sent me*" (John 6:38).

"*I press on toward the goal to win the prize for which God has called me heavenward in Christ Jesus*" (Philippians 3:14).

"*Though you have not seen him, you love him; and even though you do not see him now, you believe in him and are filled with an inexpressible and glorious joy, for you are receiving the goal of your faith, the salvation of your souls*" (1 Peter 1:8–9).

Lord Jesus, You came down from heaven to do the will of the Father who sent You, not to do Your own will. Help me direct all my energy to knowin and doin the Father's will. May the hope of gettin to heaven inspire me to do what must be done every day to get there, so that all the way to heaven can be a taste of heaven itself. Let all the distractions and disappointments that come from doin my own will decrease. Your word instructs me that the wicked will not inherit the kingdom of heaven; neither the sexually immoral, idolaters, adulterers, prostitutes, homosexual offenders, thieves, the greedy, drunkards, slanderers, nor swindlers (see 1 Corinthians 6:9–10). May all the downward-thrustin energies of the culture of death be occasions for greater reliance on You and the power of Your divine mercy and love to transform me. Help me to press on toward the goal that the Father has called me to, heavenward livin with You. May Thy kingdom come and the Father's will be done, on earth as it is in heaven, today and every day . . . Thank You, Jesus . . . Amen.

The Means — Holiness

"The kingdom of God is not a matter of eating and drinking, but of righteousness, peace and joy in the Holy Spirit, because anyone who serves Christ in this way is pleasing to God and approved by men" (Romans 14:17–18).

"The kingdom of God is not a matter of talk but of power" (1 Corinthians 4:20).

"The saints show us the way to the kingdom of heaven, the way of the Gospel radically lived. At the same time, they support our serene certitude that every created reality finds its fulfillment in Christ and that through Him, the world will be presented to God the Father fully renewed and reconciled in love" (Pope John Paul II, Homily, November 21, 1999).

Lord, help me to be holy. Make me a model of human-ity renewed by divine love. Increase within me the presence of righteousness, peace, and joy in the Holy Spirit. Help me live the Gospel. I want to serve You in this way, making progress on the path of holiness, so I can be pleasing to You and approved by men in the sense of being a credible, courageous witness, not a politically correct people-pleaser. Increase a hunger within me for the fruit of the Holy Spirit to be more present and active in my daily consciousness and contacts — more love, joy, peace, patience, kindness, goodness, faithfulness, gentleness, and self-control. Help me to crucify the sinful nature with its sinful passions that I might live by the Holy Spirit and keep in step following the Holy Spirit's lead. Let the witness of my life show Your power shining through my weakness, speaking the language of love, the language of heaven. The kingdom of God is not a matter of talk, but power — the power of Your love shining in my life through the way I live — through holi-ness. Lord, help me to be holy for real, a model of humanity renewed by divine love. Praise to You, Lord Jesus . . . Amen.

Eternal Life — Now

"I tell you the truth, whoever hears my word and believes in him who sent me has eternal life and will not be condemned; he has crossed over from death to life" (John 5:24).

"Your forefathers ate the manna in the desert, yet they died. But here is the bread that comes down from heaven, which a man may eat and not die" (John 6: 49–50).

"If anyone is in Christ he is a new creation; the old has gone, the new has come!" (2 Corinthians 5:17).

Lord Jesus, when I think about eternal life it brings up the whole issue of dying. Jesus, conquer my fear of death so that the life You offer me now can take root in my heart. Help me to hear Your word and believe in the Father who sent You, so that eternal life will not only be a thing of the future, but have a positive impact on me now. Help me know the power of hope — what it means to cross over from death to life, now and every day! Jesus, let the 'now' of eternal life empower me to live with less fear and more freedom — less fear of dying and more freedom for living. My forefathers ate manna in the desert, yet they died. You are the bread that comes down from heaven which I may eat and not die. May the promise of this truth keep me in communion with You, makin me a new creature. Let the old thinkin and feelin dominated by fear decrease a little more every day and eventually be gone; let the new life that You are come to me and stay with me forever. Thank You, Jesus . . . Amen.

84

Suicide — Overcome

"God created man for incorruption, and made him on the image of his own eternity" (Wisdom 2:23, RSV).

"In you, O LORD, I have taken refuge; let me never be put to shame. Rescue me and deliver me in your righteousness; turn your ear to me and save me. Be my rock of refuge, to which I can always go; give the command to save me, for you are my rock and my fortress . . . For you have been my hope, O Sovereign LORD, my confidence since my youth. From birth I have relied on you; you brought me from my mother's womb. I will ever praise you" (Psalm 71:1–3, 5–6).

"You were taught, with regard to your former way of life, to put off your old self, which is being corrupted by deceitful desires; to be made new in the attitudes of your minds; and to put on the new self, created to be like God in true righteousness and holiness" (Ephesians 4:22–24).

Heavenly Father, I know there's people out there right now who don't know what it means to have You for their refuge; people who are overwhelmed by shame, hatin themselves and even thinkin about endin it all. Turn Your ear to them and save them. Let them know they were created for incorruption and made in the image of Your eternity. Soothe them with this truth and with Your love. Be their rock of refuge to which they feel they can always go. Give the command and save them. Open their hearts to You to be their rock and fortress — protect them from the overwhelming feelings and thoughts that are makin them think of suicide. Be their hope and confidence; help them to rely on You and inspire them to put off the old self and old ways of thinkin and feelin that are corruptin them with deceitful and destructive desires. Make them new in the attitudes of their mind — to put on the new self, created to be like You. Father, in Jesus' name I pray . . . Amen.

Sexuality — God's Plan

"I tell you that anyone who looks at a woman lust-fully has already committed adultery with her in his heart" (Matthew 5:28).

"'Haven't you read,' he replied, 'that in the beginning the Creator 'made them male and female,' and said, 'For this reason a man will leave his father and mother and be united to his wife, and the two will become one flesh'?" (Matthew 19:4–5).

"Do you not know that your bodies are members of Christ himself?... Do you not know that he who unites himself with a prostitute is one with her in body? For it is said, 'The two will become one flesh.' But he who unites himself with the Lord is one with him in spirit. Flee from sexual immorality. All other sins a man commits are outside his body, but he who sins sexually sins against his own body. Do you not know that your body is a temple of the Holy Spirit, who is in you, whom you have received from God? You are not your own; you were bought at a price. Therefore honor God with your body" (1 Corinthians 6:15–20).

Lord Jesus, according to Your teaching, a lustful look towards another person is itself a sin against the sixth commandment committed in the heart. In a culture that has little or no respect for the sacredness of the human person and body, give me a whole new inner vision. Purify my heart, my mind, my body, and my soul and take control of all these different faculties and functions so I can submit them to the Father's plan and have a new way of seein the human body. Help me to know and care about the Father's plan for my body, the bodies of others, and the gift and responsibility of sexuality. Give me a healthy and holy love and respect for my body, myself, and the persons and bodies of others. Bless all the many people who hate themselves and their bodies, whatever the reason might be. Bless all people with same-sex attractions to submit themselves and their bodies to the Father's plan. Beyond the obvious and important realm of procreation, convict me of the unitive dimension of sex — that a man and woman leave their parents to be united with each other and become one flesh in Christ through the sacrament of marriage. Please help all couples, young and old, single and married, to have a renewed knowledge, conviction, appreciation, and respect for this context as the only true context for sexual activity — God's plan for sex. Protect me from the overwhelmingly powerful attractions of the many different forms, expressions and activities of sexual impurity and sexual immorality. Make me feel the holiness of sexuality through a living knowledge that my body is a temple of the Holy Spirit, so I can be truly grateful for and responsible with this powerful and beautiful gift, and honor You with my body . . . Alleluia . . . Amen.

86

Vices — Virtues

"Whatever is true, whatever is noble, whatever is right, whatever is pure, whatever is lovely, whatever is admirable – if anything is excellent or praiseworthy – think about such things" (Philippians 4:8).

"Make every effort to add to your faith goodness; and to goodness knowledge; and to knowledge self-control; and to self-control, perseverance; and to perseverance, godliness; and to godliness, brotherly kindness; and to brotherly kindness, love" (2 Peter 1:5–7).

"As God's chosen people, holy and dearly loved, clothe yourselves with compassion, kindness, humility, gentleness and patience. Bear with each other and forgive whatever grievances you may have against one another. Forgive as the Lord forgave you. And over all these virtues put on love, which binds them all together in perfect unity" (Colossians 3:12–14).

Holy Spirit, in the midst of a culture that is infested with toxic mental pollution, help me to think about whatever is good and excellent, what is right and pure, lovely and admirable. Increase my faith and add to my faith goodness, to goodness knowledge, to knowledge self-control, to self-control perseverance, to perseverance godliness, and to godliness brotherly kindness. As these inner qualities become more dominant by the transformation and renewal of my mind, may they be expressed as I live them out every day. Clothe me with compassion, kindness, humility, gentleness, and patience. Be with me, Holy Spirit, that I will have the inner strength to bear the burdens of my brothers and sisters, family members, friends, and strangers, and to forgive as the Lord has forgiven me. Over all these virtues help me to always put on love, which binds all the virtues in a perfect union. Come, Holy Spirit . . . Amen.

87

Church — Community

"The church throughout Judea, Galilee and Samaria enjoyed a time of peace. It was strengthened; and encouraged by the Holy Spirit, it grew in numbers, living in the fear of the Lord" (Acts 9:31).

"Do not cause anyone to stumble, whether Jews, Greeks, or the church of God – even as I try to please everybody in every way. For I am not seeking my own good but the good of many, so that they may be saved" (1 Corinthians 10:32–33).

"God placed all things under his feet and appointed him to be head over everything for the church, which is his body, the fullness of him who fills everything in every way" (Ephesians 1:22–23).

Lord Jesus, continue to bless Your Church and help me to love the Church. Grant Your Church abundant blessings of peace. Strengthen the children of the Church and encourage them in the Holy Spirit. Increase our numbers and increase our holiness living in the fear of the Lord. Expand my heart to embrace all the many different people, cultures, and circumstances, causing no one to stumble. Bless our Holy Father, the Pope, Your vicar on earth, to continue leading us in bringing the Gospel to the heart of the contemporary culture, building the civilization of love. Help me to be less concerned about seeking my own good and set my heart on fire with love and concern for the good of others in the Church, that they may be saved. God the Father placed all things under Your feet and appointed You to be head over everything for the Church — Your Body. Make me love and submit myself to this authority and share more fruitfully in the fullness of who You are through the gift and mystery of Your Church; You who fill everything in every way, who lives and reigns with God the Father, in the unity of the Holy Spirit, world without end . . . Amen.

New Creation — New Culture

"Behold, I will create new heavens and a new earth. The former things will not be remembered, nor will they come to mind" (Isaiah 65:17).

"If anyone is in Christ, he is a new creation; the old has gone, the new has come!" (2 Corinthians 5:17).

"When I began to think seriously of perfection I knew that to become a saint one had to suffer much, always aim at perfection and forget one's self. I saw that one could be a saint in varying degrees, for we are free to respond to Our Lord's invitation by doing much or little in our love for Him; that is, between the sacrifices He asks. Then, just as before, I cried: 'I choose everything; My God, I do not want to be a saint by halves. I am not afraid to suffer for Your sake; I only fear doing my own will, so I give it to You and choose everything You will'"(St. Thérèse of Lisieux, Story of a Soul).

Lord Jesus, hope makes me look forward to new heavens and a new earth. Renew my heart and mind and help me contribute towards the building of a new culture. Heal my memory and set me free from remembering former things that prevent me from trusting You. Protect me from the attack of these destructive thoughts when they come to mind. How deep I need to be in You Jesus; anyone in You becomes a new creation. Help me to be in You and to stay in You, Jesus, and with You contribute to the building of a new culture. Like Your saints, help me to think seriously about perfection; help me to know that to become a saint I must suffer much, always aiming at perfection and forgetting myself. Help me to respond to Your invitation by choosing to do much for love of You. Help me to live the Gospel without compromises and half measures. Transform my fear of suffering for You into generous willingness to suffer for You and with You. Prevent me from doing my own will; strengthen my decisions to always choose everything You will. St. Thérèse, pray for me. Amen . . .

'One, Timmy, One, One'

"Christ Jesus our hope" (1 Timothy 1:1).

Lord Jesus, You are my hope. The culture of death causes so many hearts to be hopeless and discouraged, to be deprived of the true value, meaning, purpose, and sacredness of life, to be disheartened, to be turned away from all that is authentically beautiful, true, and good with no joy. Lord Jesus, You are my hope. Lord, hear my prayer for those whose hearts are crushed by disappointment and who have no hope. Lord, may the power of hope that comes from knowing You by experience lift them up; may the power of hope that comes from choosing You lift me up; may the power of hope that comes from the presence of Your Holy Spirit give us all the courage to do the Father's work, by faith, and be the difference in a culture dominated by appearances. Give me a pure heart, a good conscience, and a sincere faith to fulfill the goal of all Your commands — love; make me a vital contributor to the building of the civilization of love...Thank You, Jesus...Amen.

No Disappointment

"My soul is weary with sorrow; strengthen me according to your word. Keep me from deceitful ways; be gracious to me through your law. I have chosen the way of truth; I have set my heart on your laws" (Psalm 119:28–30).

"Hope does not disappoint us, because God has poured out his love into our hearts by the Holy Spirit, whom he has given us" (Romans 5:5).

"When I have failed I will be careful not to lose heart and I will think that sometimes God permits this to happen so that I may become more humble and entrust myself more wholly to his loving care. After any fault I will make a profound act of humility and then begin again, as cheerfully as ever, smiling as if God had just caressed me, kissed me and raised me with his own hands – and I will set out once more, confident, joyful, 'in the name of the Lord.'" (Blessed Pope John XXIII).

Lord, when I hope in Your word, the weariness and sorrow that come from disappointment vanish like smoke in the wind! Keep me from deceitful ways and help me always to make the difficult choice for the truth, keeping my heart set on Your ways, hoping in Your word. Your way for me is the way of love, and this increases my hope in You which does not disappoint. Your love poured into my heart by the Holy Spirit protects me from all disappointment by giving me the power to "bounce back" from every failure of my expectations of myself or of others, to "bounce back" from every discouragement arising from lost opportunities or anything else that would threaten the joy of my hope in You. When I fail, I will not lose heart. Help me to make an act of humility so that the joy of "bouncing back" — beginning again — will set me out once more on the path of Your way for me, confident and joyful, tramplin down all traces of disappointment with the joy of being loved by You. Amen!

CHAPTER X

Love

The Greatest Commandment

"One of the teachers of the law came and heard them debating. Noticing that Jesus had given them a good answer, he asked him, 'Of all the commandments, which is the most important?' 'The most important one,' answered Jesus, 'is this: "Hear, O Israel, the Lord our God, the Lord is one. Love the Lord your God with all your heart and with all your soul and with all your mind and with all your strength." The second is this: "Love your neighbor as your self." There is no commandment greater than these'" (Mark 12:28–31).

"Because of the increase of wickedness, the love of most will grow cold" (Matthew 24:12).

Lord Jesus, in the midst of a noisy world, a noisy culture, and therefore a noisy inner world resulting with a divided heart, help me to lay a solid foundation for keepin the first part of the greatest commandment — help me to hear. Attune my mind to the sound of Your voice, that I might follow You. Bless my hearin You, and anoint my followin You, so that I may be renewed in lovin You. Pull together all the fragmented and scattered parts of my heart, so I can learn to love You with all my heart and all my soul, to love You with all my mind, and to love lovin You with all my strength! Yes, Lord Jesus, form me and reform me in the symphony of love that I might be more in tune with the rhythms and harmonies that are necessary for lovin my neighbor as myself. Grant me an enlightened love and respect for myself, so that I can love and respect my neighbor. In lovin and respectin my neighbor, deepen my communion with You and make it clear that it's all You, Jesus — it's all about You, Jesus. In the midst of an intense increase of wickedness in the cultures of the world causing the real meaning and practice of love to be confused and grow cold, make me burn with a raging blaze of love in who I am and through what I do, that I might be pleasing to You and a blessing to all. Thank You, Jesus . . . Amen.

The Greatest of These

"The greatest among you will be your servant. For whoever exalts himself will be humbled, and whoever humbles himself will be exalted" (Matthew 23:11–12).

"These three remain: faith, hope and love. But the greatest of these is love" (1 Corinthians 13:13).

"St. Philip [Neri] is one of the saints most familiar to me... O my good father Philip, you understand me even if I do not put my thoughts into words. Time is drawing on; where is that faithful copy of you I was to have made of myself?... O teach me the principles of your mystical school, for the education of the soul, so that I may profit by them: humility and love. I need great concentration of mind, Blessed Philip, pure and holy gaiety and enthusiasm for great works" (Blessed Pope John XXIII).

Lord Jesus, put in my heart a hunger for greatness in all that I do. Give me the loving heart of a generous servant. Protect me from being attracted to positions of high rank and power that can produce attitudes of arrogance and superiority, whether it be in Church or community, school or business, or among family and friends. Show me how to humble myself out of love for You. Captivate me with Your love and the joy of being lifted up by You — the amazing experience of being exalted through the mystery and extravagance of Your love. Increase within me faith, hope, and the greatest of all, love. Let Your teachings on love, which were embraced by Your saints, become familiar to me and rein in me as a major source of inspiration. Let the powerful combo of humility and love break down all traces of pride and self-seeking, producin within me an abundance of joy and enthusiasm for great works. Alleluia . . . Thank You, Jesus . . . Amen.

To the End

"The plans of the LORD stand firm forever, the purposes of his heart through all generations" (Psalm 33:11).

"Jesus knew that the time had come for him to leave this world and go to the Father. Having loved his own who were in the world, he now showed them the full extent of his love" (John 13:1).

"More than ever, today's world has a need to rediscover the meaning of life and death in the perspective of eternal life. Outside of it, modern culture, born to exalt man and his dignity, is paradoxically transformed into a culture of death, because without the horizon of God, he finds himself as a prisoner in the world, overwhelmed by fear, and unfortunately, gives way to multiple personal and collective pathologies" (Pope John Paul II, Angelus Message, November 3, 2002).

Lord Jesus, grant me the grace to know from deep down in my bones that the plans of the Lord stand firm forever. In the midst of a cultural context where nothin lasts — neither products, styles of clothin, nor music, neither relationships nor hardly anything else — create within me a hunger for "4-ever". Let the purposes the Your heart energize me and instruct me in the everlastin ways of the Father. Lord Jesus, when You knew that the time had come for You to pass from this world to the Father, You loved Your apostles to the end; You loved Your disciples to the end; You loved all peoples to the end; You loved me to the end. May this love "to the end" — "all the way" — burn in my heart, to purify my heart and condition my whole person to walk in the everlastin ways of Your love. Help me to rediscover the meaning of life and death in the perspective of eternal life. Free me and keep me free from bein a prisoner overwhelmed by fear, so that the personal and collective pathologies incarceratin the world through the culture of death can be overcome by my commitment to life, and by my defense of life, through my contributin towards buildin the culture of life, the culture of freedom, the culture of peace, and the civilization of love. Yes, Lord Jesus ... Amen!

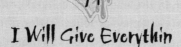

I Will Give Everythin

"The sluggard's craving will be the death of him, because his hands refuse to work. All day he craves for more, but the righteous give without sparing." (Proverbs 21:25–26).

"Go sell everything you have and give to the poor, and you will have treasure in heaven. Then, come, follow me" (Mark 10:21).

"Give, and it will be given to you. A good measure, pressed down, shaken together and running over, will be poured into your lap. For with the measure you use, it will be measured to you" (Luke 6:38).

"I will give everything to Jesus, and when I have nothing to give I will give him this nothing" (St. Thérèse of Lisieux).

Lord Jesus, help me to know and believe that to love is to give. May I come to know who I really am through makin a sincere gift of myself, more and more every day. Clear away all traces of selfishness and laziness, and replace them with generosity and zeal. Increase my inward decision to give of myself and expand my heart to be generous, and make me be like the righteous who give without sparing — who give without limit. Help me to live the radical nature of the Gospel in my daily life, startin with givin some of what I have to the poor. Increase within me a sense of the treasure in heaven in proportion to my generosity towards others. Let me see the value of Your teachin, that the measure I use in my givin will be measured to me in my receivin. Therefore, Jesus, help me to be generous with my love, with the givin of myself and what I have use of in this world. Help me work towards gradually givin my all. And when I feel I have nothin to give, Jesus, help me trust and love You so much that I will give You even this nothin. Thank You, Jesus . . . Amen.

95

A Broken, Humbled Heart

"Because of all my enemies, I am the utter contempt of my neighbors; I am a dread to my friends – those who see me on the street flee from me. I am forgotten by them as though I were dead; I have become like broken pottery" (Psalm 31:11–12).

"The sacrifices of God are a broken spirit; a broken and contrite heart, O God, you will not despise" (Psalm 51:17).

"Scorn has broken my heart and has left me helpless; I looked for sympathy, but there was none, for comforters, but I found none. They put gall in my food and gave me vinegar for my thirst" (Psalm 69: 20–21).

"The LORD is close to the brokenhearted and saves those who are crushed in spirit" (Psalm 34:18).

O God, when my spirit is broken and crushed by sorrow, when failure has reduced my strength, when I get so worn down from the weight of it all, when I feel forgotten as though I were dead, like a piece of broken glass all over the floor, please, reveal within me the truth that a true sacrifice to You is a broken spirit. Help me not to waste my sufferin. Please shine within me the truth that You will not despise or reject a broken, contrite, and humbled heart. Help me not to hold back from You during these difficult and crushin moments. Help me find a way to offer myself to You. May Your love increase within me a sense of the meanin and value of sufferin from Your perspective. During these difficult times, grant me to have a sense of Your presence; let me feel the nearness of You. I trust in Your word, which reveals that You are close to the brokenhearted and that You save those whose spirits are crushed (see Psalm 34:18). Come Lord, with Your power, and rescue me in the mystery of Your saving love. Amen . . .

96

Wounds of Love

"He heals the brokenhearted and binds up their wounds" (Psalm 147:3).

"He was pierced for our transgressions, he was crushed for our iniquities; the punishment that brought us peace was upon him, and by his wounds we are healed" (Isaiah 53:5).

"I saw a Lamb, looking as if it had been slain, standing in the center of the throne, encircled by the four living creatures and the elders" (Revelation 5:6).

"Tell me about everything, be sincere in dealing with me, revealing the wounds of your heart; I will heal them, and your suffering will become a source of your sanctification" (Jesus to St. Faustina, The Diary, #1487).

Lord Jesus, physical, mental, and emotional hurts are so difficult to get over. In a culture that finds no meanin and value in sufferin, it's even more difficult to move beyond these hurts. It even seems impossible to see these wounds as somehow connected to love. Jesus, let the light of Your divine revelation shine on me. May the fire of Your love burn an opening in my heart, causin me to experience the bindin up of my wounds. Instill within me a sense of security, confidence, stability, and peace as a result of communion with You who were pierced for my transgressions, You who were crushed for my iniquities, You who took upon Yourself the punishment that brings peace to the world, You by whose wounds I am healed. Strengthen me through the vision of Your wounds, shinin like jewels in the inner sanctuary of heaven, wounds of love, completely healed and transformed, and yet completely open as a means for the healin and transformation of my wounds and all the wounds of all peoples and nations. Help me be sincere in revealin my wounds to You, tellin You everything. Jesus, heal them. Jesus, make my sufferin be a source of my sanctification. Jesus, I trust in You. Amen . . .

God is Love

"Let us love one another, for love comes from God. Everyone who loves has been born of God and knows God. Whoever does not love does not know God, because God is love" (1 John 4:7–8).

"No one has ever seen God; but if we love one another, God lives in us and his love is made complete in us" (1 John 4:12).

"We know and rely on the love God has for us. God is love. Whoever lives in love lives in God, and God in him" (1 John 4:16).

O God, what a mystery You are. While no one can see You or understand You, You reveal Yourself in the most simple and basic way — love. You are love, plain and simple. You are love with all its complexities and challenges. You are love, so beautiful — deeper than the sea and higher than the sky. Fill me with love that comes from You; fill me with the love that is You. Strengthen me and condition me to love because when I love I am born of You; show me how the experience of love brings a real knowledge of You. Let the union of human love and divine love captivate my mind and heart and body and soul to the degree that when I do not love, I will realize that I do not know You because You are love. Help me live in the communion of love. No one has ever seen You, but when I love others and others love me, You live in me, You live in them, and we enjoy a communion that is for real and forever — love will be complete. Bring about the completion of love through the perfection of my loving — make me whole and keep me holy. Help me to rely on the love You have for me and all peoples, for You are love. Remind me always that when I live in love, I live in You and You live in me. Amen ... Alleluia ...

Mother of Love

"He went down to Nazareth with them and was obedient to them. But his mother treasured all these things in her heart" (Luke 2:51).

"This child is destined to cause the falling and rising of many in Israel, and to be a sign that will be spoken against, so that the thoughts of many hearts will be revealed. And a sword will pierce your own soul too" (Luke 2:34–35).

"When the wine was gone, Jesus' mother said to him, 'They have no more wine.' 'Dear woman, why do you involve me?' Jesus replied. 'My time had not yet come.' His mother said to the servants, 'Do whatever he tells you'" (John 2:3–5).

"Near the cross of Jesus stood his mother . . . When Jesus saw his mother there, and the disciple whom he loved standing nearby, he said to his mother, 'Dear woman, here is your son,' and to the disciple, 'Here is your mother.' From that time on, the disciple took her into his home" (John 19:25, 26–27).

Mother Mary, Mother of Love, help me to love Jesus more and more every day, that I might treasure in my heart all He said and did; that I might be willin to accept and embrace all the challenges that come my way; that I might be ever more willin to love. Pray for me, so that when my heart is pierced by the necessary sufferings that come with livin the Gospel, these sufferings will bring me and keep me close to Jesus. As you stood close to Jesus in the most difficult moment of His earthly life, as He hung dying on the cross, help me to stand close by Jesus in the sufferings of others. Pray for my heart, for an inner increase of courage, that I might be able to stand strong in love. As you anticipated the needs of the young couple at the wedding of Cana and brought their needs to Jesus, in your loving, motherly care look after my needs and help me to look after the needs of others; and when I am confronted with conflict, stress and situations that manifest no apparent solution, help me always to bring them to Jesus and be inspired by your command to do whatever Jesus tells me, trustin in God's miraculous and providential power to alleviate each and every need. At the foot the cross Jesus transferred His love for you through His command to the beloved disciple John. From that time on, John took you into his home. Mother Mary, Mother of God, Mother of Love, be my mother now and always. Amen.

99

Love Alone

"If I speak in the tongues of men and of angels, but have not love, I am only a resounding gong or a clanging cymbal. If I have the gift of prophecy and can fathom all mysteries and all knowledge, and if I have a faith that can move mountains, but have not love, I am nothing. If I give all I possess to the poor and surrender my body to the flames, but have not love I gain nothing" (1 Corinthians 13:1–3).

"These three remain: faith, hope and love. But the greatest of these is love" (1 Corinthians 13:13).

"If anyone obeys his word, God's love is truly made complete in him" (1 John 2:5–6).

"My only desire now is to love Jesus even to folly. Yes, I am drawn by love alone … I am guided by self-abandonment alone, and need no other compass, no longer knowing how to ask for anything with eagerness except that God may do His will completely in my soul" (St. Thérèse of Lisieux , Story of a Soul).

Lord Jesus, it all boils down to love, love alone. Somehow, if I was able to do the most amazin things, miracles and martyrdom included, but did not have love, I would be nothin. Increase within my life all the virtues and most especially the greatest of all virtues — love. Pour out Your love into my heart through the Holy Spirit and help me obey Your word. You said, "If you love me you will obey what I command" (John 14:15). Let Your love be made complete in me a little more every day by obeying what You command. Help me, Jesus, to walk as You did, to conduct myself as You did — to live as You did. Inspire me to love You even to folly, like a fool, beyond good sense and normal prudence. Like Your saints, guide me along the ways of divine providence and self-abandonment so the Father's will can be done completely in my life with great love. Thank You, Jesus . . . I love You Jesus . . . Alleluia . . . Amen . . . Amen . . . Amen . . .

The Civilization of Love

"I will praise you, O LORD, among the nations; I will sing of you among the peoples. For great is your love, higher than the heavens; your faithfulness reaches to the skies" (Psalm 108:3–4).

"For God so loved the world that he gave his one and only Son, that whoever believes in him shall not perish but have eternal life" (John 3:16).

"A new command I give you: Love one another. As I have loved you, so you must love one another. By this all men will know that you are my disciples, if you love one another" (John 13:34–35).

"Build the civilization of love! . . . Do not be afraid to be the saints of the new millennium. With Christ, holiness – the divine plan for every baptized person – becomes possible" (Pope John Paul II, Meeting with Syrian Youth, Damascus, Syria, May 7, 2001).

eavenly Father, Your love is great, higher than the heavens. Please set my spirit free so I can sing of You and Your love among the nations, now and forever. Father, so great is Your love for the world, includin our modern culture which distorts and perverts the true meaning of love, that You sent Jesus so that whoever believes in Him shall not perish but have eternal life. May we be overtaken by the love of Jesus and spread that love wherever we go in the light of His truth and compassion for all. Father, please help us be obedient to the new commandment given by Jesus. Help us to love one another as He has loved us. By this love, all peoples, all nations, and all cultures will know that we are His disciples. May our communion and partnership with Jesus, who is eternally young, make us a new generation of builders — the young, the not so young, the old — everybody! Energize us to build the civilization of love, a culture marked by authentic freedom and peace. Help us not to be moved by fear or violence, but rather by the urgency of genuine love. Like Your servant Pope John Paul II, may we be steeped in prayer through the power of the Holy Spirit, givin You our all every day, clingin to Jesus through His word, His mysteries the sacraments and the immaculate prayers of His and our holy Blessed Mother Mary. Father, make us the saints of the new millennium! Conquer our pride and fear with the perfect love of Your beloved Son, our Lord and Savior Jesus Christ, who lives and reigns with You and the Holy Spirit, most high, most holy and supreme God, all-good, highest good, wholly good, who alone are good; to You we render thanksgiving, all praise and all glory, now and forever . . . Amen . . . Amen . . . Amen . . . Alleluia!!!

TRADITION

Prayers U Should Know by ♥

The Sign of the Cross

In the name of the Father, and of the Son, and of the Holy Spirit. Amen.

The Apostles' Creed

I believe in God, the Father almighty, creator of heaven and earth; and in Jesus Christ, his only Son, our Lord; who was conceived by the Holy Spirit, born of the Virgin Mary, suffered under Pontius Pilate, was crucified, died, and was buried. He descended to the dead; the third day he rose again from the dead. He ascended into heaven and sits at the right hand of God, the Father almighty; from thence he shall come to judge the living and the dead. I believe in the Holy Spirit, the holy catholic Church, the communion of saints, the forgiveness of sins, the resurrection of the body, and life everlasting. Amen.

The Lord's Prayer (Our Father)

Our Father, who art in heaven, hallowed be thy name. Thy kingdom come. Thy will be done on earth, as it is in heaven. Give us this day our daily bread, and forgive us our trespasses, as we forgive those who trespass against us, and lead us not into temptation but deliver us from evil. Amen.

Hail Mary

Hail Mary, full of grace. The Lord is with thee. Blessed art thou among women, and blessed is the fruit of your womb, Jesus. Holy Mary, Mother of God, pray for us sinners, now and at the hour of our death. Amen.

Glory Be

Glory be to the Father, and to the Son, and to the Holy Spirit. As it was in the beginning, is now, and ever shall be, world without end. Amen.

Invocation of the Holy Spirit

Come Holy Spirit, fill the hearts of your faithful, and kindle in them the fire of your love. Send forth your Spirit and they shall be created. And you shall renew the face of the earth.

Let us pray: O God, who instructed the hearts of the faithful by the light of the Holy Spirit, grant us, in the same Spirit, to savor what is right, and always to rejoice in his consolation. Through Jesus Christ our Lord. Amen.

Memorare

Remember, O most gracious Virgin Mary, that never was it known that anyone who fled to your protection, implored your help, or sought your intercession was left unaided. Inspired by this confidence I fly unto you, O virgin of virgins, my

Mother. To you do I come, before you I stand, sinful and sorrowful. O Mother of the Word Incarnate, despise not my petitions, but in your mercy, hear and answer me. Amen.

The Rosary

(Taken From *Praying the Rosary: With the Joyful, Luminous, Sorrowful, & Glorious Mysteries*, by Michael Dubruiel & Amy Welborn)

Mysteries of the Rosary

The Joyful Mysteries
(Prayed on Mondays and Saturdays)

The Annunciation to Mary
The Visitation of Mary
The Nativity of Our Lord
The Presentation of the Lord
The Finding in the Temple

The Luminous Mysteries
(Prayed on Thursdays)

The Baptism of the Lord
The Wedding Feast at Cana
The Preaching of the Kingdom of God
The Transfiguration of the Lord
The Institution of the Eucharist

The Sorrowful Mysteries
(Prayed on Tuesdays and Fridays)

The Agony in the Garden

The Scourging at the Pillar
The Crowning with Thorns
The Carrying of the Cross
The Crucifixion of Our Lord

The Glorious Mysteries
(Prayed on Wednesdays and Sundays)

The Resurrection of Our Lord
The Ascension of Our Lord
The Descent of the Holy Spirit
The Assumption of the Blessed Virgin
The Coronation of Mary as Queen of Heaven

Fátima Prayer

O my Jesus, forgive us our sins, save us from the fires of hell, lead all souls to heaven, especially those who have most need of your mercy. Amen.

Hail, Holy Queen

Hail, holy Queen, Mother of Mercy, our life, our sweetness, and our hope! To thee do we cry, poor banished children of Eve; to thee do we send up our sighs, mourning, and weeping in this valley of tears. Turn then, most gracious advocate, thine eyes of mercy toward us, and after this, our exile, show unto us the blessed fruit of thy womb, Jesus. O clement, O loving, O sweet Virgin Mary!

V. Pray for us, O Holy Mother of God.
R. That we may be made worthy of the promises of Christ.

Concluding Rosary Prayer

Let us pray: O God, whose only begotten Son, by his life, death, and resurrection, has purchased for us the rewards of eternal life, grant, we beseech thee, that meditating upon these mysteries of the Most Holy Rosary of the Blessed Virgin Mary, we may imitate what they contain and obtain what they promise, through the same Christ Our Lord. Amen.

Act of Contrition

O my God, I am heartily sorry for having offended you, and I detest all my sins, because of your just punishments, but most of all because they offend you, my God, who are all good and deserving of all my love. I firmly resolve, with the help of your grace, to sin no more, and to avoid the near occasions of sin. Amen.

Act of Faith

O my God, I firmly believe that you are one God in three divine Persons, Father, Son, and Holy Spirit; I believe that your divine Son became man and died for our sins, and that he shall come to judge the living and the dead. I believe these and all the truths that the holy Catholic Church teaches, because you have revealed them, who can neither deceive nor be deceived.

Act of Hope

O my God, relying on your almighty power and infinite mercy and promises, I hope to obtain pardon for my sins, the help of your grace, and life everlasting, through the merits of Jesus Christ, my Lord and Redeemer.

Act of Charity (Act of Love)

O my God, I love you above all things, with my whole heart and soul, because you are all-good and worthy of all love. I love my neighbor as myself for the love of you. I forgive all who have injured me and ask pardon of all whom I have injured.